Automation, Innovation and Economic Crisis

T0384160

The fourth industrial revolution is developing globally, with no geographical centre. It is also taking place at enormous speed. This development will shape the workplaces of the future, which will be entirely different from the workplaces created by the first, second and third industrial revolutions. Industry created the industrial worker. The knowledge society will create a new type of "industrial worker", the knowledge worker. While the third industrial revolution was concerned with the digitalization of work, in the fourth industrial revolution, robots will bring about the informatization of work. Many of these robots will be systematically connected, such that they can obtain updated information and learn from their own and others' mistakes. The way we work, where we work, what we work on, and our relationships with our colleagues and employers are all in a state of change. The workplace of the future will not necessarily be a fixed geographical location, but may be geographically distributed and functionally divided.

In his book, Jon-Arild Johannessen argues that a "perfect" social storm occurs when inequality grows at a catastrophic rate, unemployment increases, job security is threatened for a growing number and robotization takes over even the most underpaid jobs. Thus, the ingredients for a perfect social storm will be brought forward by cascades of innovations that will most likely lead to economic and social crises and he argues that it is reasonable to assume that it will only take a small spark for this social storm to develop into a social revolution.

Jon-Arild Johannessen holds a Master of Science from Oslo University in History. He holds a Ph.D. from Stockholm University in Systemic Thinking. He is currently professor (full) in Leadership, at Kristiania University College, Oslo, and Nord University, Norway. He has been professor (full) in Innovation at Syd-Danske University, Denmark. He has been professor (full) in Management at The Arctic University, Norway. At Bodø Graduate School of Business, Norway, he had a professorship (full) in Information Management. At the Norwegian School of Management he has been professor (full) in Knowledge Management. He has written more than 200 international papers on innovation, knowledge management and leadership. He has been author/co-author of 30 books.

Routledge Studies in the Economics of Innovation

The Routledge Studies in the Economics of Innovation series is our home for comprehensive yet accessible texts on the current thinking in the field. These cutting-edge, upper-level scholarly studies and edited collections bring together robust theories from a wide range of individual disciplines and provide in-depth studies of existing and emerging approaches to innovation, and the implications of such for the global economy.

Automation, Innovation and Economic Crisis
Surviving the Fourth Industrial Revolution
Jon-Arild Johannessen

The Economic Philosophy of the Internet of Things
James Juniper

For more information about this series, please visit: www.routledge.com/ Routledge-Studies-in-the-Economics-of-Innovation/book-series/ECONINN

Automation, Innovation and Economic Crisis

Surviving the Fourth Industrial Revolution

Jon-Arild Johannessen

Routledge
Taylor & Francis Group

LONDON AND NEW YORK

First published 2018 by Routledge

2 Park Square, Milton Park, Abingdon, Oxfordshire OX14 4RN

52 Vanderbilt Avenue, New York, NY 10017

Routledge is an imprint of the Taylor & Francis Group, an informa business

First issued in paperback 2020

British Library Cataloguing in Publication Data
A catalogue record for this book is available from the British Library

Library of Congress Cataloging in Publication Data
Names: Johannessen, Jon-Arild, author.
Title: Automation, innovation and economic crisis : surviving the fourth industrial revolution / Jon-Arild Johannessen.
Description: Abingdon, Oxon ; New York, NY : Routledge, 2018. | Series: Economics of innovation | Includes bibliographical references and index.
Identifiers: LCCN 2018001648 | ISBN 9781138488601 (hardback) | ISBN 9781351039864 (ebook)
Subjects: LCSH: Robots--History--21st century. | Globalization--History--21st century. | Technological innovations--History--21st century.
Classification: LCC TJ211 .J544 2018 | DDC 330.9001/12--dc23
LC record available at https://lccn.loc.gov/2018001648

ISBN: 978-1-138-48860-1 (hbk)
ISBN: 978-0-367-59049-9 (pbk)

Typeset in Times New Roman
by Taylor & Francis Books

Contents

List of figures   vii
Acknowledgements   viii
Preface   ix

1 Trends towards feudal capitalism   1
Introduction 1
Analysis and discussion 3
Conclusion 12

**2 Globalization: the emergence of "Mamounia", the new
global nation**   17
Introduction 17
The exercise of power: totalitarian capitalism 19
Financial capital's globalization 22
Mamounia: the new global nation 28
Conclusion 32

3 Robots and informats will cause economic and social crises   38
Introduction 38
Robots and informats: economic and social crises 39
Innovation: herd behaviour and economic bubbles 43
Destructive wealth creation: transformation of social systems 48
Conclusion 53

4 Aspects of a policy architecture for the fourth industrial revolution   57
Introduction 57
The economic subsystem 59
The political subsystem 63
The cultural subsystem 66

The social subsystem 69
Conclusion 72

5   Concepts   **78**

Index   99

Figures

1.1   The fourth industrial revolution   3
1.2   Six concepts that summarise the developments of the fourth
      industrial revolution   7
1.3   Robotization   9
1.4   A typology of knowledge workers in the fourth industrial
      revolution   11
1.5   Aspects of the future workplace: a systemic overall perspective   13
1.6   What constitutes the fourth revolution, and some assumed
      consequences   14
2.1   Globalization   19
2.2   The differences between trade, trade agreements and free trade
      agreements   24
2.3   Mamounia: the new global nation   29
2.4   Mamounia and the global power system   33
3.1   Robotization   40
3.2   A typology of working life in the fourth industrial revolution   42
3.3   Herd behaviour, economic bubbles and economic and social
      crises   46
3.4   Technological trends that will create our future up until 2050   53
3.5   Robotization and the fourth industrial revolution   54
4.1   A policy architecture for the fourth industrial revolution   60
4.2   Aspects of a policy for the economic subsystem in the fourth
      industrial revolution   63
4.3   Aspects of a policy for the political subsystem in the fourth
      industrial revolution   66
4.4   Aspects of a policy for the cultural subsystem in the fourth
      industrial revolution   69
4.5   Aspects of a policy for the collaborative system in the fourth
      industrial revolution   72

Acknowledgements

I want to thank the staff at Routledge, who helped me to make this book much better than I could have done by myself. Especially I want to thank the editor, Kristina Abbotts.

Preface

The book is divided into four chapters and a chapter on concepts used in the book. In Chapter 1 we discuss the question: What constitutes the fourth industrial revolution? The objective with the question is to understand the fourth industrial revolution. The findings in Chapter 1 are an analytical model that shows aspects of the factors which constitute the fourth industrial revolution, together with some of the key consequences of the fourth industrial revolution.

The question discussed in Chapter 2 is: How does globalization constitute an aspect of the fourth industrial revolution? The objective is to understand and explain how globalization affects, and is affected by, the fourth industrial revolution. The findings in Chapter 2 are that the global power system is fostering a totalitarian form of capitalism and controlling the global knowledge economy via financial capital in a new nation, "Mamounia", which consists of the One Per Cent of the population in the world.

The question discussed in Chapter 3 is: How does robotization constitute an aspect of the fourth industrial revolution? The objective is to conceptualize some of the consequences of the fourth industrial revolution. The findings in Chapter 3 are linked to two conceptual models explaining the question studied and the objective of the chapter.

Due to extreme economic inequality, the fourth industrial revolution may develop in such a way that it could be detrimental to organizations and nations. The question discussed in Chapter 4 is: Which overall policy can be developed so that the fourth industrial revolution will lead to greater value creation for the benefit of an increasing number of people?

The objective is to design a policy architecture that can reduce the development of strong tensions and conflicts in the fourth industrial revolution. The findings in Chapter 4 are 17 policy interventions that are systemically linked. This comprises six policy interventions for the economic subsystem; three policy interventions for the political subsystem; three policy interventions for the cultural subsystem and five policy interventions for the collaborative system.

1   Trends towards feudal capitalism

Introduction

The most important invention of the first industrial revolution was the steam engine. The second industrial revolution spawned the combustion engine, and the third industrial revolution the computer. The fourth industrial revolution will see the rise of robots. These robots will be integrated into all types of products, both known and unknown (Valnazarova & Ydesen, 2016).

The fourth industrial revolution is being driven forward by robotization and globalization (Schwab, 2016). Robots with artificial intelligence are of a qualitatively different order than the wave of automated machines we saw in the third industrial revolution (Brynjolfsson & Saunders, 2013). These robots can be programmed to sense their surroundings, understand what is happening, adapt their behaviour in accordance with this understanding and learn from their actions, without any need for reprogramming (Brynjolfsson & McAfee, 2011; 2014).

Obviously, we do not know how the fourth industrial revolution will progress, but we can apply historical insight and innovation theory, as well as our understanding of economics, in order to predict some likely developments.

The fourth industrial revolution is developing globally, with no geographical centre (Dickinson, 2016). It is also taking place at enormous speed. The spread of computers from the 1950s onwards was limited by many factors, including the world situation, East–West tensions and the absence of a well-developed internet (Rogers, 1962). No such limiting factors apply to the spread of robot technology. This spread is exponential, is taking place worldwide and is systemically connected (Reinert & Rogoff, 2009).

The fourth industrial revolution can be summed up in six concepts. We have described three of them above: the rate of spread, which is driven by cascading innovations; the global area of impact, which is driven by globalization; the systemic links, which are driven by robotization and informatization. The three other concepts are linked to the three concepts listed above. These concepts are threshold value, feedback and time-lag. Threshold value is relevant because some sectors will join the fourth industrial revolution only once a certain threshold value has been exceeded, not unlike the situation where a dam bursts once a specific threshold is exceeded. Feedback may be understood as meaning that some people understand what is about to happen before others. The former group react and adapt to the new development before others do so. Accordingly, the former group gain an advantage over the others, who will come on board later. Time-lag means that the more one is part of the fourth industrial revolution, the less of a time-lag one will be willing to accept. For example, this time-lag may be the time that elapses between sending a message and receiving a response. One of the consequences of this is that a relatively long time-lag will function psychologically as information stress.

These six concepts – rate of spread, global impact area, systemic links, threshold value, feedback and time-lag – function both as descriptions of what is happening in the fourth industrial revolution, and are also used here as explanations of the consequences of the fourth industrial revolution.

The knowledge society is mushrooming out of the global economy, and artificial intelligence and robotization are the key drivers (Frankish, 2014). This development will shape the workplaces of the future, which will be completely different from the workplaces created by the industrial revolution (Barrat, 2015). Industry created the industrial worker. The knowledge society will create a new type of "industrial worker", the knowledge worker (Case, 2016). The knowledge worker is not a homogeneous category, but consists of different types of worker, distinguished by level of competence, type of function performed and manner of thinking (Brynjolfsson & McAfee, 2014).

The five elements that emerge here – the knowledge society; globalization; robotization; the future workplace; and the knowledge worker – are all based on a revolutionary innovation that will change the basic assumptions underlying all social systems (Brynjolfsson & McAfee, 2011). Innovation is the overarching driver of the new knowledge society that we are seeing foreshadowed today, according to Brynjolfsson and Saunders (2013).

This chapter explores the following research problem: What constitutes the fourth industrial revolution?

The questions that we investigate in order to answer this research problem are the following:

- How does the knowledge society constitute an aspect of the fourth industrial revolution?
- How does globalization constitute an aspect of the fourth industrial revolution?
- How does robotization constitute an aspect of the fourth industrial revolution?
- How does the workplace of the future constitute an aspect of the fourth industrial revolution?

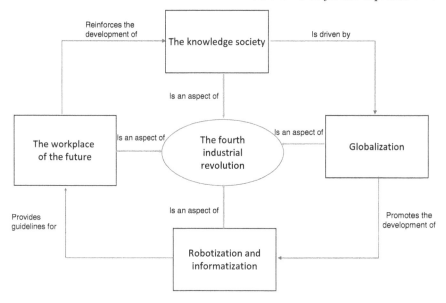

Figure 1.1 The fourth industrial revolution

This introduction is visualized in Figure 1.1, which also shows how we have structured this chapter.

Analysis and discussion

In the following, the four elements in Figure 1.1 will be analysed and discussed.

The knowledge society

Several simultaneous trends characterize developments towards the knowledge society. Innovation is without doubt one such tendency that will increase (Gans, 2016). However, it is debated whether the market alone will manage to accommodate the major challenges we face (Ford, 2016: 283). These challenges include migration from areas of famine, drought, poverty and an unworthy life, and people fleeing war, crises and conflicts (Johnson, 2014). Another challenge also related to migration is the growing climate crisis (Smil, 2012). A third challenge is the rising unemployment among people who lack the necessary education and expertise demanded of the fourth industrial revolution (Ford, 2016). A fourth challenge is the issue of economic disparity, the ever-widening gap between rich and poor, both globally and nationally, as well as in urban areas (Piketty, 2016).

Economic, psychological and social security will come under strong pressure (Bauman, 2013; Sennett, 1999, 2003, 2013). The use of terms such as "the working poor" (Shipler, 2005) and "the precariat" (Standing, 2014b; Savage, 2015) signal clear indications of this trend. The middle class, the backbone of capitalism in the 20th century, will be marginalized and decimated with the emergence of the fourth industrial revolution in the 21st century (Wacquant, 2007, 2009a, 2009b; Savage, 2015; Standing, 2014b). Even those with a long university education will experience job insecurity – many will have educated themselves into unemployment (Gupta et al., 2016; Coates, 2016).

A "perfect" social storm occurs when inequality grows at a catastrophic rate, unemployment increases, job security is threatened for a growing number and robotization takes over even the most underpaid jobs in, for instance, the service industries (Ford, 2016; Wacquant, 2009b).

Paradoxically, productivity increases for those who have jobs, due to the new robotic technology, and those working in high-tech manufacturing will enjoy higher wages. However, the conflict between those with well-paying jobs in high-productivity occupations, and those with poorly paid jobs and the unemployed, will increase sharply (Savage, 2015; Standing, 2014b). In addition, social tensions will increase due to a gradual disconnection between productivity and pay (Pilger, 2016). Thus, although productivity and profits increase, wages relatively decrease (Piketty, 2014; Ford, 2016). If this gradual disconnection is correct, then the social contract will slowly come under stress and be weakened (Goodman, 2015). The disconnection between productivity and wages will have many social, economic and political consequences. Inequalities will grow and expectations of a better future for people and their children will lessen. Despair and desperation will grow side by side with apathy (Savage, 2015; Standing, 2014b; McGill, 2016). Thus, the ingredients for a perfect social storm will be brought forward by cascades of innovations that will most likely lead to economic and social crises (Johannessen, 2016). It seems reasonable to assume that it will only take a little spark for the social storm to develop into a social revolution (Petras et al., 2013).

The underlying main driver behind this development is information and communication technology (ICT). Moore's Law states that every 18 to 24 months, computer power is doubled (Thackray, 2015). From 1950 up until today, this development has affected people's lives, organizations' development, nations' wealth creation and the dynamics of globalization (Webster, 2004). All levels of society have been affected by these developments. The rapidity of the pace of change even affects us right down to the level of our thoughts – what we think and believe about our own and our children's future (Pilger, 2016; Savage, 2015). One example of these developments is the recent explosive growth in electric cars, which in the not too distant future could be the only vehicles permitted in traffic; a little further into the future, these electric cars may be self-driven. Thus, such a minor aspect of current technological development may result in our cities being less polluted. Consequently, people may move back to the inner cities, resulting in new re-structuring and re-organization of urban areas; this could even result in the rich living in the city centres while the poor move into the countryside (Wacquant, 2007).

Technological developments will very likely lead to new educational offerings, new jobs requiring different skills, and new functions in institutions and organizations (Pilger, 2016).

Then comes the paradox. Those with relatively long university educations will also find that their jobs are taken over by robots. This could prove to be those who thought they were very secure in their jobs, such as lawyers, doctors, radiologists, journalists, teachers, financial clerks, etc. Any jobs that involve instrumental, linear, repetitive processes that can be predicted by some logical algorithm will eventually be threatened by the "super-intelligent" robot (Pilger, 2016; Savage, 2015; Ford, 2016). The reason for this threat is that the classic relationship between productivity, wages and consumption will collapse (Ford, 2016: xvii). The explanation is that the increased productivity to a lesser extent will go to salaries, but find its way to profits (Piketty, 2014). What we will see is that although productivity increases, salaries will not increase at the same rate (Sprague, 2015).

Globalization

Among the factors that drove forward globalization were China's new economic orientation towards the West around 1988 and the fall of the USSR (1991) that followed that of the Berlin Wall in 1989. This led to more than 1.5 billion people being incorporated in the capitalist economy (Stigliz, 2003, 2007; Swider, 2015; Dickinson, 2016). Another essential prerequisite for globalization was the new ICT and Internet that functioned as an integrative mechanism (Brynjolfsson & Saunders, 2013).

There are two main aspects of globalization. The first is that more and more people are drawn into wealth creation, education and out of extreme poverty (Smil, 2012; Valnazarova & Ydesen, 2016). The second is that some areas are depleted, and poverty becomes entrenched (Rodrik, 2011; Standing, 2014b; Rojecki, 2016). Mason (2015: ix–xxi) describes this development by referring to the country Moldova in Eastern Europe which has remained an economic backwater despite globalization.

One of the results of globalization is obvious – the competition economy as we know it from economics textbooks no longer exists (Roat, 2016). In the present day, it is the major international funds and large international corporations that largely control developments (Charnock & Starosta, 2016; Petras & Veltmeyr, 2001). Figuratively, these operate as feudal vassals setting limits for competition and wage conditions; this new brand of capitalism in the fourth industrial revolution is often referred to as "feudal capitalism". These three factors, financial capital, neo-liberalism and feudal capitalism, are radically transforming the international working class (Rojecki, 2016; Charnock & Starosta, 2016). People are seeking better lives for themselves and their families where there are jobs, and where wages are relatively higher (Olds, 2004; Petras et al., 2013). This is resulting in large-scale global migration (Dickinson, 2016), such as from Africa to Europe, but also migration within regional and national areas, such as from rural to urban areas in Europe and the United States (Varoufakis, 2015; Dickinson, 2016).

Those that govern financial capital and have control over production are interested in minimizing labour costs by transferring them across the globe (Chomsky, 2012; Varoufakis, 2015; Petras et al., 2013). In other words, the relative wages share of value creation is reduced while profits are increased (Piketty, 2016; Ford, 2016; Petras & Veltmeyr, 2011; McGill, 2016). Over time, such a development will not only weaken the working class, but also the middle class (Coates & Morrison, 2016; Gupta et al., 2016), which will lead to tensions and conflicts (Goodman, 2015). One consequence of this may be a rebellion against the elite (Petras & Veltmeyr, 2001, 2011).

A simple inference from prospect theory suggests that this elite will try to maintain their positions, their share of the wealth creation and the benefits they have already achieved (Kahneman & Tversky, 2000). This theory, for which Kahneman and Tversky won the Nobel Prize, states, in brief, that people will spend more energy preserving their positions, income and status, than fighting to achieve these benefits (Adriaenssen & Johannessen, 2016). The rebellion mentioned above may come from either the right or left side of the political spectrum, or take on a completely different form than we can imagine today (Mason, 2015; Petras et al., 2013).

There were good financial results over the globe in China, India, Indonesia, Australia, South Korea, Europe, the US, parts of Africa and large parts of South America (Mason, 2015). However, this economic progress collapsed after the financial crisis (Gaskarth, 2015). The question is whether neoliberalism has outlived its usefulness, and the global economy needs to be re-started using a different economic approach (Wiedemer, 2015; Petras & Veltmeyr, 2013). The new economic system that now manifests itself is a form of feudal capitalism, where large funds and major international corporations downplay competition and focus on stability.

One of the results of the ongoing crisis in the world economy is that economic growth has stagnated. Economic growth will stagnate *for the next fifty years* according to OECD (OECD, 2014). Meanwhile, inequalities are exploding both globally and nationally (Piketty, 2014, 2016; McGill, 2016).

Figure 1.2 shows the social mechanisms which drives the fourth industrial revolution.

Robotization

Skilled work is being increasingly carried out without skilled workers, but by robots (Ford, 2016). The robots will take over both knowledge jobs, such as automated legal services, automated cleaning services and self-checkout machines in shops (Brynjolfsson & Saunders, 2013; Winfield, 2012).

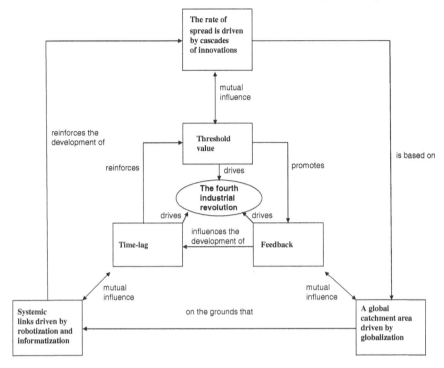

Figure 1.2 Six concepts that summarise the developments of the fourth industrial
revolution

The use of robots will change the nature of activities in the following professions: medical, legal, dentistry, teaching, nursing, etc. (Charnock & Starosta, 2016; Valnazarova & Ydesen, 2016). In the not so distant future,
robotization of all the service professions and all the knowledge occupations
will be an actuality (Coates & Morrison, 2016; Susskind & Susskind, 2015).
The main trend is that all the functions that can be digitized will require less
human work (Case, 2016).

Odense, a city on the island of Fyn in Denmark is well known inter-
nationally by the name of "Robotic Valley". In June 2016) there were 80
companies working with design, construction and assembly of various types
of robots. The prognosis for this type of industrial activity is predicted (in this
case, Odense) to have an annual growth of 15 per cent. However, it is also
reported that there are a lack of skilled workers who can occupy these types
of jobs, despite the fact that there is growing unemployment. The types of
jobs that are in demand in the robotic cluster in Odense require specialized
skills acquired through short, medium and long educations.[1] This would
indicate that the fourth industrial revolution's main component, robots, will
affect the education market considerably at all levels of competence (Coates &
Morrison, 2016; Susskind & Susskind, 2015).

The use of robots in industry is nothing new. For instance, Volvo and other car makes have used them for decades (Winfield, 2012). So what's new? What's new is the fall in the price of robots, their application, the distribution and the use of nanotechnology to increase their functionality (Mataric, 2007). Tesla's factory is an example of how the use of robotization has skyrocketed in auto production. Some of the advantages of robotization are speed, precision, resilience and strength in the execution of work processes (Abd, 2017). Nursing in hospitals and nursing homes, where nursing work is often physically tiring, is one particular domain where increased robotization could make daily work less tiring and more effective. In the near future, robots will also be able to "see" the needs of patients (Xie, 2017), and intervene where necessary. The robots' "eyes" will soon be developed so that they can "see" and understand better than the human eye (Abd, 2017). In the near future, the robots' "eyes" will be able to detect movement, signs, articulations, grimaces and emotional changes (Bleuer et al., 2017). When this happens, many of the jobs in several of the service occupations will disappear or at least be transformed (Susskind & Susskind, 2015).

Robotization will in all probability lead to an explosion of innovation in all, absolutely all, professions, hobbies and functions (Antonelli, 2001; Wilson, 2017). These cascades of innovations will, as we know from innovation theory (Christensen, 2016), destroy established jobs and develop new professions with new competencies (Case, 2016; Johannessen, 2016).

In such a process, the entire education system will change in relation to the requirements of robotization and informatization (Gupta et al., 2016). Such innovations will not only lead to the destruction of established jobs and develop new professions, but will also lead to temporary economic crises (Johannessen, 2016). Out of the crises, large and small, there will emerge a flock of new entrepreneurs (Ford, 2016), who figuratively may be understood as a flock of "phoenix-birds".

Cascades of innovations and the flock of "phoenix-birds" will take off once standards are drawn up for the construction of robots' operating systems (Wilson, 2017). Then entrepreneurs and innovators can concentrate on developing "Lego parts" that fit into an overall design of the individual robots (Zhao et al., 2017).

While innovators with their new inventions create gaps in the market, then entrepreneurs rush in and fill these gaps (Johannessen, 2016). The prerequisite for this development is that there exists a design logic based on the global info-structure, where production, distribution and consumption are integrated into a cohesive system (Lima, 2017). In addition, it will be a condition that standardization creates a modular logic where individual local developers can design and produce their own "Lego parts", which fit into the overall design (Gershuny & Fisher, 2014; Wilson, 2017). Specialized knowledge workers will design and develop "nano" robots which fit into a larger design (Zhao et al., 2017), not unlike some functions in a car engine, or functions in a computer (Brynjolfsson & McAfee, 2014).

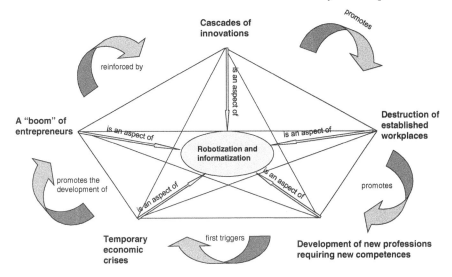

Figure 1.3 Robotization

These new "Lego parts" or functions do not need to be owned by the individual client. The client acquires access to these new functions, for example, via "cloud robotics" in analogy to "cloud-memory" functions that already exist. "Cloud robotics" is data-power in the form of, for example, nano-robot technology that is designed for modular "Lego logic", and is located in the "cloud" and rented by the client. In this way, the costs of robots are lowered considerably because they can be put into mass production. Clients gain access to advanced robotic technology through leases. They can further rent newer levels of computing power through various leases, from free cost, such as the lowest level in a dropbox, to a relatively high rental rate for accessing the desired data-power in various "Lego parts".

What expertise will be in demand in the robotic industry? Design, technology, creativity and innovation will be the winners in this new knowledge explosion (Brockman, 2010: 10–14; Lima, 2017; Xie, 2017). The design, maintenance and modification of robots will require a highly specialized level of expertise (Case, 2016; Zhao, 2017).

Figure 1.3 shows a visualization of the developments that have been analysed and discussed above.

The workplace of the future

Knowledge workers are those who mainly deal with production and the distribution of information (Jemielniak, 2014: 11–22). We can imagine that knowledge work can be divided into two groups. One group are those who are trained for instrumental and linear thinking.

These knowledge workers often have tasks that are repetitive and predictable, for instance, technicians and engineers of various kinds. The second group consists of those who think creatively and systemically, for instance, various types of designers. Designers may work on software design, design of robotic applications, but also the more traditional understanding of design, such as furniture design, fashion design, etc. Designers, working systematically, are expected to create innovative solutions to challenges and problems (Gans, 2016).

The knowledge worker will emerge as the central resource of the fourth industrial revolution (Ford, 2016: xvi). The knowledge worker may be classified into at least four different types (Garza, 2013; Christensen, 2016). Those who have 3–5 years of university education will probably be the new "industrial workers" in the fourth industrial revolution (Ford, 2016; Jemielniak, 2014). Their work will be characterized by instrumental and linear thinking (Catmull, 2014). Many of those with university educations will also take on temporary project positions as self-employed with no relationship to one specific employer. These individuals will be characterized by creative, innovative and systemic thinking (Catmull, 2014). The second main type of knowledge worker will be those with a PhD or equivalent. These may also be divided into two groups. One group, those with T-shaped skills, the knowledge geeks, will be included in the fourth industrial revolution. T-shaped skills means, as the letter T suggests visually, both breadth and depth of knowledge. These knowledge geeks are also characterized by instrumental and linear thinking (Christensen, 2016). Essentially, these individuals will be involved with the maintenance of robots, and they will be highly specialized in programming and robot design.

The second type at the PhD level will be the independent experts. Their mode is creative, innovative and systemic thinking (Catmull, 2014). The knowledge worker in the fourth industrial revolution, in other words, will be a multi-faceted animal, ranging from the traditional "industrial worker" to the independent expert (Susskind & Susskind, 2015).

In Figure 1.4 we have developed a typology of the knowledge workers in the fourth industrial revolution.

The new "hirelings" or precariat go from job to job, and only value their work in so much as it puts bread on the table. They have no fixed relationships to employers but work on short term contracts. This new class, says Standing (2014b: vi–ix), don't relate to 1970s trade union thinking, or to socialist ideology. They rebel against established institutions, comprising both the right and left of the political spectrum (Ross, 2016). The rebellion is aimed upwards towards the elite, irrespective of political leaning (Standing, 2014a). This class is characterized by uncertainty, insecurity, lack of confidence about the future and a perception of being oppressed over a long period (Sennett, 1999, 2013). This oppression has an upper threshold value. When this threshold value is exceeded, the rebellion against their unworthy lives will be ignited. This class of distressed people often show their fury by extremist attitudes and

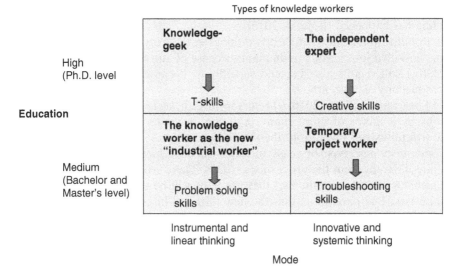

Figure 1.4 A typology of knowledge workers in the fourth industrial revolution

behaviour (Standing, 2014b). Standing (2014b: vii) says: "Across the world, there is an energy building around the precariat." The trend in the industrialized countries (OECD) reinforces the hirelings or the precariat as a class, as more and more are being pushed out of the labour market, or pushed into poorly paid, and meaningless jobs.

Those who feel that their jobs are insecure, and have little or no expectations of a better future, also experience a growing frustration in relation to globalization and robotization (Srinivasa, 2017; Noonan & Nadkarny, 2016; McGill, 2016). This is also occurring in poorly paid service jobs (Ross, 2016).

The 2000s has witnessed a new type of capitalism, a transition from nation-state industrial capitalism, to global capitalism with feudal structures, which may be termed feudal capitalism.

The manufacturing jobs that in the 1980s demanded 2,000 industrial workers, skilled and mostly unskilled, require today 140 skilled workers with special expertise (Ford, 2016: 9). This description is derived from a production facility in California; if it gives a fairly accurate picture generally, then this tells us a lot about what we can expect in the future. Competition for jobs will increase, without necessarily an increase in wages, because there will be so many competing for the jobs that wages will be lowered even further. Profits will grow, and inequalities will increase exponentially (Piketty, 2016). Robotization will result in some of the production be reintroduced to the old industrialized countries from the low-cost countries, but the jobs will not follow. The rationale is that labour will be in less demand, because the robots will have replaced human labour (Monbiot, 2016). Thus, in the period between when the jobs were re-located to low-cost countries in Asia, and the production taken "home" again to domestic industries, i.e. re-shoring, something has happened (Rojecki, 2016).

Robotization leads to at least two things at the workplaces. Firstly, many of the unskilled jobs become redundant, because of automation. Secondly, many of the skilled jobs also become superfluous because robotization increases productivity significantly.

The example Ford (2016: 9) refers to in California leads to a reduction of jobs by a factor of more than 10. If this becomes a characteristic of the fourth industrial revolution, then we have problems. This would most likely result in a new type of mass unemployment, which would be something quite different from the crisis of the 1930s. There will be a great increase in unemployment despite the fact that new jobs will be created and productivity increases. The paradox is that the new jobs will largely be so-called project jobs based on part-time work (Petras & Veltmeyr, 2001, 2011). This development will also apply to highly educated people with university education (Monbiot, 2016). The California story mentioned above could be a forerunner of even further developments such as fully automated manufacturing, which will only need a few highly specialized engineers to maintain the robots. This could lead to the social contract being completely pulverized and feudal capitalism becoming a reality.

This predicted mass unemployment will most likely develop social mechanisms to hide unemployment, such as "citizen salaries" combined with lifelong learning.

Re-shoring will also result in lower transport costs, because the goods can be produced nearer the market. This would be advantageous regarding the reduction of emissions into the environment, but would negatively affect the transport industry.

The other aspect of this development is that automation will also be established in developing countries, such as China, Vietnam, Indonesia and India. With low capital costs, low labour costs and an extremely flexible labour force, which often live in large dormitories outside the factories (Ford, 2016: 12), re-shoring will come to a halt. Competition from developing countries would again threaten jobs in the industrialized world. Thus, after a brief period of re-shoring, the developing countries, by investing in informatization and robotics, will out-compete the jobs in the industrialized countries.

In such a scenario, the OECD area will develop mass unemployment that will likely lead to social conflicts that may threaten the stability of these countries (Petras & Veltmeyr, 2011).

The analysis above is visualized in Figure 1.5.

Conclusion

The problem for discussion in this chapter was: What constitutes the fourth industrial revolution?

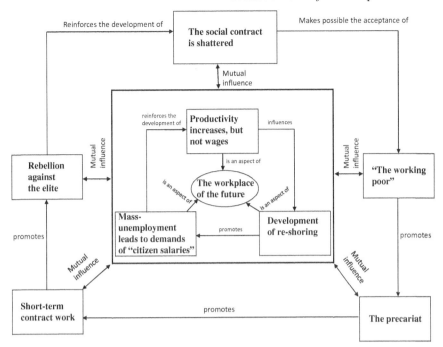

Figure 1.5 Aspects of the future workplace: a systemic overall perspective

In the fourth industrial revolution, thinking will evolve from linear to interactive or disruptive. While the third industrial revolution was about the digitalization of work, in the fourth industrial revolution, robots will bring about the informatization of work. Many of these robots will be systematically connected, such that they can obtain updated information and learn from their own and others' mistakes.

The way we work, where we work, what we work on and our relationships with our colleagues and employers are all in a state of change. The workplace of the future will not necessarily be a fixed geographical location, but may be geographically distributed and functionally divided. In this context, "functionally divided" means that the workplace of the future will largely consist of temporary project-base roles with people performing different functions for different employers. Working hours will also become individualized, i.e., the 9–5 working day will be consigned to history and people will work as if they were self-employed entrepreneurs, although in reality they will be working as subcontractors for various clients. Management in this scenario will be about coordinating individualized, distributed workplaces, and coordinating workers who will largely be self-managing within the framework of fixed contractual targets.

The answer to the problem is presented in Figure 1.6, which is a revision of Figure 1.1.

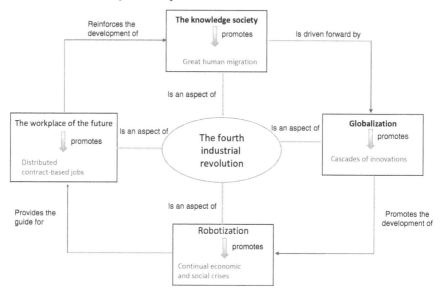

Figure 1.6 What constitutes the fourth revolution, and some assumed consequences

Note

1 *Politikken* (a Danish newspaper), 10th June, 2016, p. 1.

References

Abd, K.K. (2017). *Intelligent scheduling of robotic flexible assembly cells*, Springer, London.

Adriaenssen, D. & Johannessen, J-A. (2016). Prospect theory, *Problems and Perspectives in Management* 14, 2: 84–92.

Antonelli, V. (2001). *The microeconomics of technological change*, Oxford University Press, Oxford.

Barrat, J. (2015). *Our final invention*, St Martin's Griffin, London.

Bauman, Z. (2013). *Does the richness of the few benefit us all?* Polity, London.

Brockman, J. (Ed.) (2010). *This will change everything*, Harper, New York.

Bleuer, H., Bouri, M. & Mandada, F.C. (2017). *New trends in medical and service robots*, Springer, London.

Brynjolfsson, E. & McAfee, A. (2011). *Race against the machine*, Digital Frontier Press, New York.

Brynjolfsson, E. & McAfee, A. (2014). *The second machine age*, W.W. Norton & Company, New York.

Brynjolfsson, E. & Saunders, A. (2013). *Wired for innovation: How information technology is reshaping the economy*, The MIT Press, London.

Case, S. (2016). *The third wave*, Simon & Schuster, New York.

Catmull, E. (2014). *Creativity Inc.*, Bantam Books, New York.

Charnock, G. & Starosta, G. (2016). *The new international division of labour: global transformation and uneven development*, Palgrave, London.

Chomsky, N. (2012). *How the world works*, Hamish Hamilton, London.

Christensen, C.M. (2016). *The Clayton M. Christensen reader*, Harvard Business School Press, Boston.

Coates, K.S. & Morrison, B. (2016). *Dream factories*, Dundum, London.

Dickinson, E. (2016). *Globalization and migration*, Rowman & Littlefield, London.

Ford, M. (2016). *The rise of the robots: technology and the threat of mass unemployment*, Oneworld, London.

Frankish, K. (2014). *The Cambridge handbook of artificial intelligence*, Cambridge University Press, Cambridge,

Gans, J. (2016). *The disruption dilemma*, The MIT Press, Boston.

Garza, D. (2013). *Disrupting*, Create Space, New York.

Gaskarth, J. (ed.). (2015). *China, India and the future of international society*, Rowman & Littlefield, London.

Gershuny, J. & Fisher, K. (2014). *Post-industrious society: why work time will not disappear for our grandchildren*, Center for Time Use Research, Department of Sociology, University of Oxford, Oxford.

Goodman, J. (2015). *Crisis, movement, management: globalising dynamics*, Routledge, London.

Gupta, S., Habjan, J. & Tutek, H. (2016). *Academic labour unemployment and global higher education: neoliberal politics of funding and management*, Palgrave, London.

Jemielniak, D. (2014). *The laws of the knowledge workplace*, Gower, London.

Johannessen, J-A. (2016). *Innovations leads to economic crises: explaining the bubble economy*, Palgrave, London.

Johnson, M. (2014). *Precariat, labour, work and politics*, Routledge, London.

Kahneman, D. & Tversky, A. (2000). Prospect theory: an analysis of decision under risk, in Kahneman, D. & Tversky, A. (eds). *Choices, values and frames*, Cambridge University Press, Cambridge, pp. 17–43.

Lima, P.U. (2017). *Autonomous mobile robotics: a system perspective*, CRS Press, New York.

Mataric, M.J. (2007). *The robotics primer*, MIT Press, Boston.

Mason, P. (2015). *Postcapitalism: a guide to our future*, Allen Lane, London.

McGill, K. (2016). *Global inequality*, University of Toronto Press, Toronto.

Monbiot, G. (2016). *How did we get into this mess*, Verso, London.

Noonan, N.C. & Nadkarny, V. (2016). *Challenge and change*, Palgrave, London.

OECD (2014). *Policy Challenges for the next 50 years*, OECD, Brussels.

Olds, K. (2004). *Globalization and urban change*, Oxford University Press, Oxford.

Smil, V. (2012). *Global catastrophes and trends*, MIT Press, Boston.

Petras, J. & Veltmeyr, H. (2001). *Globalization unmasked*, Zed Books, London.

Petras, J. & Veltmeyr, H. (2011). *Beyond neoliberalism: a word to win*, Routledge, London.

Petras, J., Veltmeyr, H. & Marquez, H. (2013). *Imperialism and capitalism in the twenty-first century: A system of crises*, Routledge, London.

Piketty, T. (2014). *Capital in the twenty-first century*, The Belknap Press of Harvard University Press, Boston.

Piketty, T. (2016). *Chronicles: On our troubled times*, Viking, London

Pilger, J. (2016). *The new rulers of the world*, Verso, London.

Reinert, C.M. and K.S. Rogoff. (2009). *This time it's different: eight centuries of financial folly*, Princeton University Press, Princeton.

Roat, H. (2016). *Capital and collusion: the political logic of global economic development*, Princeton University Press, Princeton.

Rodrik, D. (2011). *The globalization paradox*, Oxford University Press, Oxford.

Rogers, E.M. (1962). *Diffusion of Innovations*, Free Press, Glencoe.

Rojecki, A. (2016). *America and the politics of insecurity*, John Hopkins University Press, New York.

Ross, A. (2016). *The industries of the future*, Simon & Schuster, London.

Savage, M. (2015). *Social class in the 21st century*, Penguin, London.

Schwab, K. (2016). *The fourth industrial revolution*, World Economic Forum, Geneva.

Sennett, R. (1999). *The corrosion of character*, W.W. Norton, New York.

Sennett, R. (2003). *The fall of public man*, Penguin, New York.

Sennett, R. (2013). *Together*, Penguin, New York.

Shipler, D. (2005). *The working poor*, Vintage, New York

Sprague, S. (2015). What can labor productivity tell us about the US economy, *US Bureau of Labor Statistics, Beyond the numbers* 3, 12 (May).

Srinivasa, R. (2017). *Whose global village: rethinking how technology shapes the world*, NYU Press, London.

Standing, G. (2014a). *A precariat charter*, Bloomsbury, London.

Standing, G. (2014b). *The precariat: the new dangerous class*, Bloomsbury Academic, New York.Stigliz, J. (2003). *Globalization and its discontents*, Penguin, New York.

Stigliz, J. (2007). *Making globalization work*, Penguin, New York.

Susskind, R. & Susskind, D. (2015). *The future of professions: how technology will transform the work of human experts*, OUP, Oxford.

Swider, S. (2015). *Building China, informal work and the new precariat*, Ilr Press, London.

Thackray, A. (2015). *Moore's law*, Basic Books, London.

Valnazarova, A. & Ydesen, C. (2016). *UNESCO without borders*, Routledge, London.

Varoufakis, Y. (2015). *The global minotaur*, Zed Books, London.

Wacquant, L. (2007). *Urban outcast*, Polity, London.

Wacquant, L. (2009a). *Prisons of poverty*, University of Minnesota Press, New York.

Wacquant, L. (2009b). *Punishing the poor*, Duke University Press, London.Webster, F. (2004). *The information society reader*, Routledge, London.

Wiedemer, D., Wiedemer, R.A. & Spitzer, C.S. (2015). *Aftershock*, Wiley, London.

Wilson, M. (2017). *Implementation of robot systems*, Butterworth-Heinemann, New York.

Winfield, A. (2012). *Robotics*, OUP, Oxford.

Xie, S. (2017). *Advanced robotics for medical rehabilitation*, Springer, London.

Zhao, J., Feng, Z., Chu, F. & Ma, N. (2017). *Advanced theory of constraint and motion analysis for robot mechanisms*, Academic Press, London.

2 Globalization

The emergence of "Mamounia", the new global nation

Introduction

As a topic, globalization came to prominence in the 1980s and 1990s. Explanations for the rise of globalization include the fall of the Berlin Wall in 1989 and China's entry into world markets in the 1980s[1]. Other important factors were the emergence of modern communications technology and the Internet. International power politics became more significant, since there was much at stake when the Cold War ended following the fall of the Berlin Wall and the collapse of the Soviet Union.

New communications technology and the Internet, together with the growth in international trade, have made financial institutions into global operators. The fact that international trade reached approximately 1.5 billion additional people relatively quickly had an effect on economic development worldwide. Trade lifted many people out of poverty, including in China and India. This trend also resulted in some of the people involved in global capitalism becoming extremely wealthy. These people became members of an elite, known as the One Per Cent (Dorling, 2015). As time went on, the members of this new class adopted lifestyles that meant they could be considered a separate nation whose members were more or less exempt from their obligations in the countries in which they lived. The identity of this new One Per Cent class became linked with the notion that it is the rich who create jobs for everyone else, or that benefits and privileges for the wealthy trickle down to others. The Norwegian proverb "When it rains on the priest, the sexton also gets wet" illustrates this "trickle-down economics" (Lehmans, 2015). Such ideas led the One Per Cent and their intellectual brothers-in-arms to believe that they were entitled to certain privileges, e.g. lower taxes (Sowell, 2012).

One of the results of globalization and the emergence of this new One Per Cent was the transfer of production from countries that had become wealthy due to industrialization to parts of the world with significantly lower production costs. As time went on, this caused rich countries to become poorer in relative terms. Accordingly, one could claim that one result of the emergence of the new One Per Cent class has been to make wealthy countries poorer, while increasing the wealth of the One Per Cent to almost unimaginable levels. This trend, whereby a small number of people have become extremely wealthy, while many others have seen their jobs disappear overseas to China, Vietnam, Indonesia, India etc., triggered the emergence of forces opposed to globalization. These anti-globalization forces appeared on both sides of the political spectrum. We saw this in 2016 in the American election, where Donald Trump represented right-wing opponents of globalization, while Bernie Sanders represented their left-wing counterparts. We saw similar trends in Brexit, in Hungary, in Italy, in Austria, in France, etc. The opponents of globalization are on the advance: in some places, they are overturning governments, in others they are threatening the status quo.

Globalization puts the concept of the nation state under pressure (Martell, 2010: 1). In particular, welfare states in Europe have come under pressure. The wave of migration that occurred during the first decade of the 21st century further increased pressure on the economic system that formed the basis of the welfare state. Roughly at the same time as the emergence of globalization, a new economic philosophy developed: neo-liberalism (Eagleton-Pierce, 2016). One of the consequences of this new brand of economics was the deliberate engineering of economic disparity. Other consequences of neo-liberalism included major economic and social problems in many developing countries (Martell, 2010: 6).

Economic, cultural and political globalization, as well as the globalization of social challenges through migration, are increasingly putting pressure on nation states. One explanation for this situation is that it is becoming ever more difficult to solve these problems within the borders of individual nation states. Instead, these problems must be resolved regionally and globally. This makes it necessary to undertake political, economic and social interventions at a supranational level. This has consequences that include a reduction in the influence of democratic institutions. The power to get things done is being transferred to fora where democratic control is for the most part absent (Bauman, 2013; Chomsky, 2012).

This chapter explores the following research problem: How does globalization constitute an aspect of the fourth industrial revolution?

We have formulated three research questions in order to investigate this problem:

1   How does the exercise of power constitute an aspect of the fourth industrial revolution?
2   How does financial globalization constitute an aspect of the fourth industrial revolution?
3   How does the new global "nation" constitute an aspect of the fourth industrial revolution?

Figure 2.1 provides an overview of the introduction. Figure 2.1 also illustrates the structure of this chapter.

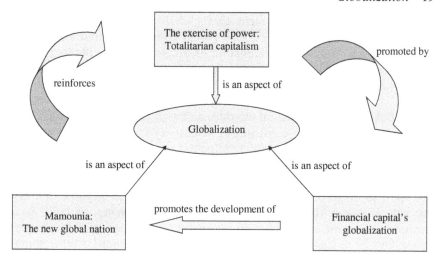

Figure 2.1 Globalization

The exercise of power: totalitarian capitalism

The United States, Russia and China have clear intentions to both threaten and actually use military force in order to achieve dominance in areas they consider to be within their sphere of influence (Chomsky 1999, 2014, 2015b, 2016). This has given rise to a strategy that is explicit in the United States, and practised in China and Russia, of initiating preventive wars for the purposes of securing national interests (Chomsky, 2004, 2015a). In this competitive global environment, international law is mere hot air, and is applied only to protect the superpowers' own interests (Chomsky, 2016). This was the case, for example, with the invasion of Iraq. It is not the case, however, that all nations have the right to conduct this kind of a preventive military strategy. According to Chomsky (2004: 239), the right to undertake such aggressive acts is reserved in general for the United States and its allies. A historian and adviser to the Kennedy administration, wrote that the invasion of Iraq had imposed on the United States: "a global wave of hatred of American arrogance and militarism."[2] The invasion of Iraq did not reduce terrorism; in fact it had quite the opposite effect. The invasion of Iraq created a new militant movement, Islamic State, of which we have subsequently borne the consequences (Cockburn, 2015).

Al Qaeda was also the result of American support for Afghan resistance to the Soviet Union during the 1980s (Burke, 2004). Both Al Qaeda and Islamic State were thus the result of deliberate American policy, even if the consequences that Americans and others ultimately had to bear were not.

Globalization has made military force, and the exercise of it, an active strategy for achieving dominance on the world's markets. This is particularly true of the United States, but Russia and China are following the same path (Raskin, 2015).

On this basis, it seems evident that globalization leads to inequality, insecure employment due to extreme global competition, and competition for lower wages resulting in a reduction of wages relative to profits (Piketty, 2014, 2016). In addition, closer relationships are developing between the business world and politics (Reich, 2009).[3] The incursion of business into politics became all the more evident when billionaire Donald Trump won the 2016 American presidential election, and with the subsequent formation of his new administration consisting of several key players from the world of business.

What then is the psychological "glue" of globalization? One economic psychological mechanism which may be important is the belief in self-interest. The spirit seems to be that what is good for the individual is good for everyone else. However, this idea, on which the capitalist system is built, is an erroneous economic and psychological construction according to Reich in his best-selling book *Supercapitalism* (Reich, 2009: viii). Amongst other things, the construction is faulty because the models it uses become in their consequences the empirical data being examined. The rationale is that if enough people use these models and this thinking, after a period of time one will find support for the models in practice. The models used thus become self-fulfilling prophecies. The faulty construction does not take into account people's sense of justice. When we see that the few are given benefits that the majority do not receive, such as tax reductions for the rich, then we are no longer willing to enter into a social contract that is based on the free market. We realise that the "free" market is not free at all but rigged for the profit of the few (Chomsky, 1999, 2015a, 2015b; Bauman, 2013). "Free" is used as a concept in this context because who wishes to be unfree? However, the free market is not as "free" as some would claim it to be. In other words, the "free" market is not so much an empirical reality but rather an ideological assumption. That is, it is a belief system and not an empirical system. Yet the free market is assumed to be an empirical fact.

According to Reich, one of the consequences of globalization is the decline of democratic capitalism and the rise of totalitarian capitalism (Reich, 2009: x). However, it is not only in China and Russia that totalitarian capitalism has taken hold, it has also manifested itself in the US and EU. Although the façade in the US and the EU may be democratic, in reality the economic system has gained an increasing influence on the political system (Chomsky, 1999, 2004; Freeland, 2013). By totalitarian capitalism, we mean that the economic subsystem has penetrated the political subsystem, dismantling democratic processes. In other words, there is much to suggest that democratic processes are being undermined because the administration of states is hampered by global financial directives.

Paradoxically, although the capitalist system has developed in a more totalitarian direction, consumers have gained greater choice of products, and many people are experiencing increased prosperity since the start of globalization in the 1980s (Reich, 2009: 7).

Managerial salaries have greatly increased since the development of totalitarian capitalism (since the 1980s). In most countries, leaders of medium-sized enterprises often receive higher salaries than the country's political leaders. In itself, this fact sends a clear signal of what is viewed as being important in society: leading a democratic country, or leading a medium-sized private business?

Both Milton Friedman (2002: 10) and Robert Reich (2009: 9), although they stand far apart on the political spectrum, claim that capitalism is a precondition of democracy. However democracy is by no means a pre-condition of capitalism. We have witnessed this in China and to some extent in Russia. China has a free market and a capitalist economy but politically is hardly what most people in the West would associate with democracy. We have witnessed the same in Chile under the military junta of 1973, in Spain under the dictator General Franco, in Italy under Mussolini, and in Germany under Hitler. The importance of capitalism as a social mechanism of democracy is most likely exaggerated.

So far, this analysis has attempted to show that capitalist enterprises and democracy are not related elements. They may well exist side by side, but capitalist enterprises can just as well exist side by side with totalitarian governments, fascist governments, military dictatorships and communist regimes. Milton Friedman and Robert Reich's assertion that capitalism is a pre-condition for democracy hardly corresponds with historical reality. However, it is perhaps not difficult to understand why they hold such an ideological assumption. It is based on the belief that capitalism promotes democratic development, which is both right and wrong at the same time.

There are many who claim that the large multinational corporations have taken over in areas where national governments were previously the key players. However, as Robert Reich correctly points out, it is rather the case that the large corporations have less influence after the increase in competition (Reich, 2009: 10). It is rather the large global investment funds that increasingly govern developments. These funds are managed by people who have only one single factor to guide their actions in financial activities: profit. If they ignore this factor, then the members of the pension funds and so on will react through their representatives at general meetings and in other decision-making forums. Thus, from being controlled by the major global corporations a more hidden form of governance is now emerging and is being exercised by those people managing the major investment funds.

The development of global capitalism is not so much controlled by a few large global corporations, but is rather dependent on a way of thinking. This "way of thinking" has many names, such as neo-liberalism, neo-conservatism and so on. However, the core of this ideology is the belief that the market solves all problems. Some of the elements of this ideology are: free trade, deregulation, common standards and privatization, etc. (Harvey, 2007; Petras & Veltmeyr, 2011).

Totalitarian capitalism has not evolved because of a few large corporations controlling developments. Rather, totalitarian capitalism is rooted in a way of thinking, where economic growth, free trade and profit are the principal modes of thought. It is the consequences of such thinking that have led the world into totalitarian capitalism. We see an unvarnished version of it in China and Russia. However, it is also evident in the EU and the United States, through, amongst other things, the invasion of other countries in order to gain control of developments or in the way the European Central Bank and the World Bank treated Greece in 2015 after a democratic election (Varoufakis, 2015).

The road to totalitarian capitalism goes via China, Russia and a form of capitalism in the West that increasingly puts profits in front of people's prosperity (Chomsky, 2014, 2015a, 2015b, 2016).

The democratic aspects of capitalism have come under pressure from several quarters, including global companies (Reich, 2009: 50). How did this happen? The growing competition brought about by globalization has put costs under pressure. Workers have had to compete with workers in other countries where the wages are low. The results may easily be seen: bankruptcies, relocation of jobs, unemployment and an unworthy life for many. In such a situation, people will often support those who say they can help them achieve a worthy life. As well, we have the scapegoat syndrome. In Europe and the US, the scapegoats are the immigrants, refugees and migrants: the "strangers" that Bauman refers to (Bauman, 2013). This is no less the case when Robert Reich in his best-selling book *Supercapitalism* says that the negative criticism of globalization "is mostly nonsense" (2009: 50). Obviously, someone who supports and is supported by the elite would argue that globalization is mainly positive. In elite thinking, capitalism is the opposite of what is described above, namely "a better life for all". Moreover, is this not what the elite have always asserted, even though we witness millions of people experiencing worse conditions in Greece, Spain, the UK, France, the US and other countries. Of course Reich's book is a bestseller! It maintains the myth that capitalism is for the benefit of all, even when millions of people in the author's own country have been shoved into unworthy lives. Robert Reich (2015) has emphatically pointed this out in his book *Saving Capitalism*. In Reich's book, he is joined by two of the heavyweights in economics, Joseph Stiglitz and Paul Krugman. However, their claims are not necessarily correct despite the fact that they are both Nobel Prize winners in economics. It may rather be the case that they are largely influenced by their own ideology.

Totalitarian capitalism is promoted by the quest for profit which is a fundamental aspect of the same capitalism that Reich, Stiglitz and Krugman are defenders of, even though their ideas place them in the centre rather than in alignment with the neo-liberalists.

Financial capital's globalization

Stiglitz, the Nobel laureate in economics, who defends capitalism says: "Globalization today is not working for many of the world's poor" (Stiglitz, 2002: 214). At the same time he says: "We cannot go back on globalization: it

is here to stay" (Stiglitz, 2002: 222). In the industrialized world, the traditional industrial workers have suffered huge losses due to globalization. On
the other hand, many, especially in developing countries, have benefited; this
applies both to a growing middle class and the industrial workers in the
developing countries who work in factories that were moved there from the
old industrialised countries.

It is primarily trade, the new technology and access to markets with cheap
goods that has meant an increase in living standards for millions of people in,
for instance, China, India, Vietnam and other countries in Asia (Giddens,
2002; Martell, 2010). The increased prosperity has also led to better health in
these countries (Gaskarth, 2015; Swider, 2015). Stiglitz (2002: 214) says that it
is not so much globalization that is the problem, but the way globalization
has been managed, and the role played by global organizations such as the
World Trade Organisation (WTO), the International Monetary Fund (IMF)
and the World Bank. However, the problem with Stiglitz's view is that he
disconnects the relationship between globalization and globalization's social
mechanisms. It is precisely these aforementioned institutions[4] in cooperation
with the major multinational corporations and the global investment funds
that have fuelled what one calls globalization. Such a disconnection between a
phenomenon and that which drives the phenomenon is like disconnecting
profits from capitalism, and then saying that capitalism is good, but that it is
the profits that destroy capitalism. Without the said institutions, globalization
is not globalization, but something quite different. This something quite different
is international trade, i.e. international trade driven by internationalization
not globalization.

The basis for international trade was bilateral trade agreements. Countries
have participated in international trade at least since antiquity, for instance,
when Alexander the Great expanded trade to Persia and parts of India. In
Roman times, the international trade expanded with the import of pepper and
other spices from Southern India (Johannessen, 2016: 9–35). Thus, globalisa-
tion and international trade are two different things. Globalization requires a
different mindset than internationalization. While internationalization was
driven by trade agreements, globalization has been fuelled by free trade
agreements, among other things. It is when supranational institutions such as
the WTO, IMF and World Bank, as well as multinational corporations and
global investment funds, operate outside national frameworks that globalization becomes different from internationalization. We have visualized the differences between trade, trade agreements and free trade agreements in Figure 2.2.

It is when financial capital has woven its network across the global markets
that globalization becomes institutionalized (Robé, 2016). With financial
capital's globalization, inequality in the industrialized world has greatly
increased (Piketty, 2014, 2016). Piketty and others have shown that globalization and free trade have led to increasing economic inequality. Against this
background, the IMF and the World Bank have modified their discourse and
now focus more on addressing poverty and growing inequality. This is

Principal distinction

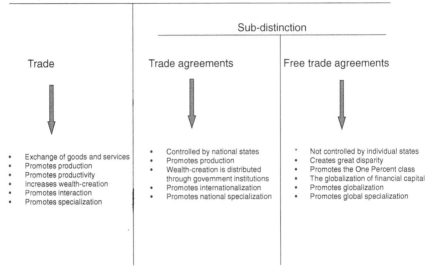

Figure 2.2 The differences between trade, trade agreements and free trade agreements

interesting to note considering that some believe they contributed to the dis-
parities in the first place. Figuratively, this may be likened to a wolf slaugh-
tering some sheep in the flock so the remaining sheep have enough pasture
between them to survive.

Market fundamentalism and the globalization of financial institutions are
important drivers of globalization (Eagleton-Pierce, 2016). Globalization is
based on a fundamentalist ideology (Petras & Veltmeyr, 2011). The problem
of globalization is not so much international trade, but rather the fact that it
is based on an ideology that promotes the welfare of some at the expense of
others (Harvey, 2007). In other words, problems arise when profit is put before
people's welfare (Chomsky, 1999; Bauman, 2013). Matters are not helped
much when the Nobel laureate in economics, Stiglitz, believes it is the management of globalization that is at fault, rather than globalization as such; and
says that "I believe that globalization can be reshaped to realize its potential
for good, and I believe that the international economic institutions can be
reshaped in ways that will help ensure that this is accomplished" (Stiglitz,
2002: 215).

Financial capital's globalization serves the interests of some, making some
people very rich (Piketty, 2014, 2016; Bauman, 2013). However, everybody
else has to endure the consequences of the decisions that are made, such as
the financial crisis that was triggered in autumn 2007 (Johannessen, 2016:
125–130). Globalization, and especially financial capital's globalization, exerts
pressure on democratic institutions in such a way that decisions reached in
national democratic forums may be likened to the "decisions" made by a

louse in a cod's gills (the louse always has to swim the same way as the fish). In the face-off between national democratic institutions and global finance, there have been few instances in which the will of the former has prevailed.

The financial crisis that was triggered in autumn 2007 is still (in 2018) the cause of major negative consequences for many. The crisis was caused by the pursuit of quick and large profits (Roberts, 2016). Instead of considering the global system as a holistic pattern of interactive individual elements, it was viewed as consisting of separate closed circuits. This has had consequences. When the rate of profit began to fall, the house of cards also collapsed (Roberts, 2016). The negative consequences had to be borne by the many people who ended up unemployed, homeless, socially declassed and social outcasts; moreover, we have witnessed the phenomenon of a disintegrating middle class. The banks and their managements were rescued by the various national governments at the expense of the taxpayers' money (Johannessen, 2016: 125–155).

Regarding the IMF, the World Bank and WTO, they of course genuinely believe that their recommendations serve everyone's interests (Stiglitz, 2002: 216). At least, this was believed until everything started to go wrong around 2007 when the financial crisis erupted. It is often the case that those who talk of "serving everyone's interests" have their own interests in mind, and the interests of those they receive their livelihoods from. It is rarely the case, if ever, that people in private or public institutions speak about their own interests or the interests of their superiors; as a rule, they argue for the interests of everyone. However, it is within their argumentation that we can find the real ideology that lies behind their reasoning. The thinking the said institutions promote is the importance of the market economy, and specifically the American variant (Stiglitz, 2002: 218–222). The benefactors of this kind of market liberalism are the economic elite (Piketty, 2014, 2016; Petras & Veltmeyr, 2011). The international financial institutions follow a logic that is distant from the ideas that people in the West associate with democracy. One aspect of Western democracy is the right of public access to information to enable informed choices. However, the international financial institutions rarely live up to such democratic ideas (Dorling, 2015). Their decisions are taken behind closed doors, and thus consequences are disconnected from their decisions. The democratic institutions lack of access means they are unable to assess the various consequences the closed-room decisions might have for people (Freeland, 2013).

Those who control global financial capital are the masters of the global universe. Global financial capital amounting to billions is moved around in digital space. The power of global financial capital is immense. The rich's capital wealth is handled by the financial elite. A few keystrokes on their part may result in the loss of hundreds of jobs one day and thousands the next (Wacquant, 2009a, 2009b). Over time, they cause the financial tectonic plates to shift resulting in millions of workers becoming unemployed so they need to look for new work. However, many of these unemployed workers do not have the necessary skills to switch to new jobs created in the global knowledge economy. These people may be termed the new "working poor" (Shipler, 2005), or the new precariat (Standing, 2014a, 2014b) in Europe and the US.

Thus, over time, financial capital's keystrokes can change the fate of millions and millions of people. Their keystrokes on their digital screens may be compared to those making a few keystrokes controlling the war machine's drones, bringing death to a small village in Afghanistan or Iraq, an urban district of Aleppo, or a side street somewhere in Libya. The fund brokers on the global stock exchanges in Hong Kong, Singapore, New York, London, Frankfurt, and so on, are the real masters of the global economic combat zone. What these people do collectively can alarm any world leader says Ferguson (2002: 279). Profit is not just *a part* of their activities. *Everything* concerns profit. Their fundamental values revolve around self-interest (Harvey, 2007). The fate of others that is decided by their keystrokes does not constitute a basis for reflection on their part (Chomsky, 1999). Of course, this does not happen because these people are evil. It happens because their actions are guided by a single factor, that of profit (Dorling, 2015; Chomsky, 2016). While self-interest and profits are the gospel of the financial elite (Mason, 2015; Chomsky, 1999; Bauman, 2013), supply and demand constitute their action programme. Their room for reflection is debit and credit. This is what drives them and makes them tick. However, the fact that others have to suffer the consequences of their speculations is not included in their calculations.

The global bond market is enormous. Between 1982 and 1997 it increased by a factor of six to $25 trillion. By 1999, the amount had grown to $34 trillion.[5] This may be understood as the economic foundation of the new nation that figuratively saw the light of day with the rise of globalization. We call this new nation Mamounia. The global bond market is worth more than the GNP of all the world's nations (Ferguson, 2002: 280–281).

Yet, the international flow of capital is nothing new. The Romans used financial capital to extract ore, trade with distant regions and lands, and conduct war (Johannessen, 2016: 9–35). Also in medieval times there were large flows of financial capital between countries. The same was the case in the 1600s and 1700s and later (Kørner, 1995: 507–521; Johannessen, 2016: 35–89). The aim then and now of trade is to make greater profits than is possible within the borders of a single country. There are few people today or in the past who oppose trade as such. However, free trade is a contentious economic topic. Free trade is related to an ideology where neoliberalism is a strong element (Petras & Veltmeyr, 2011). The fundamental idea of neoliberalism is that everyone profits when goods, services, financial capital and labour flow freely between nations (Eagleton-Pierce, 2016). It is claimed beyond doubt that trade promotes economic prosperity (Bonney, 1995). However, it is very doubtful that free trade profits everybody (Harvey, 2007). Micklethwait and Wooldridge (2000) along with several others view globalization in a largely positive light. Others beg to differ, such as the sociologist Giddens (2002) who views globalization as being very problematic for nations, families and individuals. Another sociologist, Sennett, has reached similar conclusions in several of his books (Sennett, 1999, 2003, 2009, 2013).

We already know that some people profit enormously from free trade (Ferguson, 2002: 311; Piketty, 2014, 2016). However, many workers and also those in the middle classes, especially in the old industrial nations, are unable to compete in today's world, because labour costs are lower in countries such as China, India, Vietnam, as well as other countries in Asia (Bauman, 2013; Chomsky, 2015a, 2016). UN figures (1999) showed that three of the world's richest people had greater financial resources than the sum of the gross domestic product of the poorest countries, where 600 million people live (Ferguson, 2002: 311). By 2016, income disparity still had not been reduced (Piketty, 2016).

Global financial capital steers nations towards a unified perception of what is deemed as being the correct economic policies. For instance, recently, this was evident in the case of Greece. Sixteen days after the leftist party Syriza had won the democratic election in Greece in 2015, the European National Bank withdrew their loan from the country (Mason, 2015: ix). It might be said in this context that financial capital clearly expressed its views concerning democratic processes. Greece's Finance Minister, Yanis Varoufakis, had to agree to all the conditions laid down by the European Central Bank, otherwise the country would be staring bankruptcy in the face. The lesson we can draw from the Greek case is simple: politicians do not govern Europe, financial capital does (Mason, 2015: xi). While politicians wish the best for their respective nations, financial capital wishes the best for their investments and profits, and these two goals seldom coincide. Global financial capital does not take into account national interests, but rather the logic of profit. The globalization of financial capital is particularly evident in the case of Greece. Arguably, there was and still is a Greek economic crisis. Varoufakis (2015) makes a pertinent argument when he says that the Greek crisis is only a symptom of a paradigm shift, where there is a transition from an industrial economy to a global knowledge economy. The paradigm shift concerns a transition from national industrial economy thinking, to global knowledge economy thinking.

The dominant global knowledge economy thinking from about 2000 to 2008 was that financial capital was now organized in such a way that risk had been eliminated from financial transactions. However, when risk spiralled out of control into the flaming crisis in 2007–2008 then everyone was greatly astonished. Metaphorically, the fault lay in the fact that they could not see the wood for the trees. They focused on profits and not the system as a whole, with its social, political and cultural consequences.

Financial innovation, like all other types of innovation, is not necessarily a good thing (Johannessen, 2016). In the case of the 2008 crisis, it was definitely a bad thing for most people, but not for everyone. The 2008 crisis, similar to the crisis in 1929, was not triggered because the banks were greedy, although many were. Neither was it triggered by using the wrong economic theory, although parts of the economic theory cannot cope with the run up to an economic crisis. The crisis was triggered due to new financial innovations that created such complexity that no one, absolutely no one, had knowledge of what was happening or the possible consequences.

Innovations lead to economic crises and the financial innovation we saw in the prelude to the economic crisis in 2008 was no exception (Johannessen, 2016: 125–155). One can agree with Varoufakis (2015: 21–22) who compares the capitalist system in a crisis to an injured global minotaur that reacts accordingly when profits are threatened by smashing everything in sight.

One might also say figuratively that the capitalist system is designed like the phoenix bird which sets itself alight and rises from the ashes to start a better life. Economic equilibrium is re-established in the capitalist system when it is able to rise from its own destruction. Thus, capitalism has an in-built social mechanism that drives the social system towards a crisis, but emerges anew from the same crisis. However, there are the millions of people "in the ashes" who never find their way back to the lives they had before. Many of these were tied to industrial production in the OECD area, but there were also millions of the middle classes in the West who were socially de-classed. One might say that the 2008 crisis inflicted severe damage on the middle classes – they just have not fully registered the damage yet because they are still in shock.

Mamounia: the new global nation

According to Ruggie (2016: xii), laws, regulations and business practices have changed dramatically between 2000 and today. We are at what Gladwell (2013) calls a "tipping point", where new power centres, new technologies and the absence of international laws are fostering the development of a new elite, whose members live in a new state, Mamounia. This elite is the One Per Cent, whose members are remote from most other people on the planet (Mason, 2015). In Mamounia, information and communications processes occur between the old continent and the new, which is Mamounia. The old continent consists of low-cost and high-cost countries. Low-cost countries send goods and services to high-cost countries, while high-cost countries invest in low-cost countries, as we have shown in Figure 2.3.

While institutions, laws and regulations are well developed in the old continent, they are absent in Mamounia. A transfer of wealth is occurring from the old continent to Mamounia, i.e., from local states to the One Per Cent who live in Mamounia. The One Per Cent "inhabitants" of Mamounia use the old continent's infrastructure. Most of the "inhabitants" of Mamounia live off the infostructure of the global knowledge economy. This infostructure is disengaged from the control of local states.

Historically, the nations of the old continent were the principal players on the international scene. Together with other states they created the laws and regulations and established the norms and values which were followed by individual states and in the relations between the states. However, in the

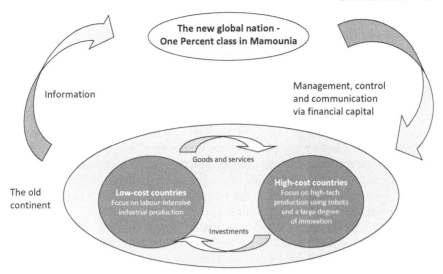

The new global nation -
One Percent class in Mamounia

Information

Management, control
and communication
via financial capital

Goods and services

The old
continent

Low-cost countries
Focus on labour-intensive
industrial production

High-cost countries
Focus on high-tech
production using robots
and a large degree
of innovation

Investments

Figure 2.3 Mamounia: the new global nation

global economy things are done differently. First, it was the large multi-national corporations that acquired a more central role. This concerned, and to some extent still does, companies such as Exxon, GE, Siemens, Unilever, Sinopec, Google, Coca-Cola, Toyota, Novartis, SAB Miller, and so on. Gradu-ally, the large investment funds also began to acquire greater importance. These include funds such as the Government Pension Fund of Norway, the Kuwait Investment Fund, and so on. These funds have no single company they deliver results to. On the contrary, they convey their results to people such as the hundreds of millions of retirees and future retirees worldwide whose pensions are invested in various funds. Normally, it is only a single guideline that guides their operations and that is the return on invested capital. Of course, guidelines and regulations may also take into consideration ethics and the protection of the environment, and so on. Nonetheless, as a rule, it is profit that is the dominant guideline. In such a situation, financial capital has gained in importance at the expense of both individual states and multi-national corporations. It may be said that there are now three players on the international scene: national governments, multinational corporations and large investment funds. This development was made possible through priva-tization, liberalization, the protection of investors and the privatization of the sovereignty of individual states. By the latter, we mean that the banks and other financial institutions have consciously created opportunities for investors to place their profits in countries with low levels of taxation, and information about the said individuals is virtually absent (Ruggie, 2016: xii). The One Per Cent class have thus been created in the wake of such developments. The One Per Cent class live apart from the 99 per cent; although they may be geo-graphically located in the various states, they live apart in the sense that they are protected by walls, fences and guards to ensure their safety. It is this One Per Cent that inhabit the new nation Mamounia. These are some of the contributing factors that are making the rich nations poorer. The same is the case concerning the multinational corporations. They operate according to a completely different logic than that of state capital. The legal challenges of these multinational corporations are also great, as we have witnessed in the case of Google whose practices have been challenged by the EU's European Commissioner for Competition, Margrethe Vestager.[6] While national states have developed a legal basis for individual companies, "international law barely recognizes the existence of multinational enterprises at all; indeed a number of scholars go so far as to describe it as invisible" (Ruggie, 2016: xiii). It is against such a background that the financial foundation of Mamounia has been developed, as well as its cultural and social foundations.

The multinational corporations are able to greatly influence the policies of national states, especially the terms and conditions that affect the individual corporations. This is partly driven by lobbying, where the corporations have huge financial muscle to influence and bring about decisions in favour of their own views. They can thus exert pressure on national governments to adopt laws that reduce the risk for the corporations, while the individual national states still have to shoulder the risk (Champeil-Desplats, 2016; Chomsky, 2016).

We have reached "the tipping point" (Gladwell, 2013), where the global economy has reached a critical threshold. Gladwell (2013: 7) points out that ideas, information and behaviour spread like viruses do. At the beginning of the global "epidemic", there was only an increasing internationalization of enterprises. The epidemic then spread exponentially like wildfire. In addition, there was the creation of that which is new, that is, an emergent[7] that created a mutation in the virus that was underlying the epidemic. This changed the direction and strength of the epidemic. The results of this epidemic are just beginning to show themselves. Firstly, we have witnessed the emergence of extreme economical inequality, political earthquakes and signs of a cultural revolution in which the political, bureaucratic and intellectual elite have become targets. Secondly, the whole process is making the rich nations poorer, and the poor nations richer. Thirdly, there has been a spike in the fear of "strangers", immigrants, refugees and other migrants. This has created political movements that are not opposed to globalization but are opposed to migration which is one of the consequences of globalization. Fourthly, internationalization has been transformed into globalization. Globalization is qualitatively different from internationalization. Internationalization is based on regular trade agreements, while globalization is increasingly based on free trade and free trade agreements (see Figure 2.2). There is a significant difference between regular trade agreements and free trade agreements. Globalization and free trade agreements create an excess of profits that contribute to building the new nation we call here Mamounia.

Mamounia is an emergent, something that is qualitatively new that has not existed in the world before. The power system of Mamounia is not anchored in any single country. The large multinational corporations and large invest-ment funds play a crucial role within this new power system. The development of the new power system has occurred without any overall plan, but resembles an epidemic in which no one knows who will be affected, when or where. Mamounia is also an emergent in the sense that there are no institutions, citizens, budgets, military system or anything we normally associate with the establishment of a new nation. Thus, Mamounia is in this sense a fiction, but it is also very real for two reasons. Firstly, Mamounia is real in the impact it has on national governments, enterprises and individuals. Secondly, Mamounia is real because the power Mamounia possesses has major consequences for national states. Yet, researchers have no analytical tools with which they can analyse the power system of Mamounia. Researchers have to rely on statistics related to the financial system's development, integration, and the management and control of financial capital. Yet, what we see happening may be described as the development of a new "world power system" (Robé, 2016: 11). Pictorially, the evolution of this power system resembles an octopus whose tentacles are reaching out across the globe. The challenge for researchers is to con-ceptualise this power system says Robé (2016: 11). This is the task we attempt here, and which is indicatively shown in Figure 2.3 and Figure 2.4.

Mamounia, and the new power system has no constitution, no geo-graphical locality, no citizens in the classical sense and no laws. Mamounia self-institutionalizes its power structures in favour of some and to the dis-advantage of others. Like a parasite, Mamounia uses its host to survive. In this way, Mamounia makes the rich nations poorer, by taking without giving. If this maladaptive parasite goes unchecked, it may end up killing its host. If the social system does not expire due to this parasite, it will nevertheless impoverish large groups in the former industrial states, who will end up de-classed, unemployed and living in fear of what the future may bring.

The power relations are developed through self-reinforcing loops. One example is the transfer of labour-intensive work to low-cost countries (Figure 2.2) due to competition focusing on labour costs. This has affected employment in the rust belt in the US, the automotive industry in Detroit, US, and in the industrial areas in Wales, and so on. Jobs disappear and are not replaced by new employment opportunities because the low-cost countries can always com-pete on labour costs. Millions of jobs have disappeared in this way from the United States (Wacquant, 2007, 2009a, 2009b). The power systems in Mamounia benefit from the competition for low labour costs, because it has an epidemic-like ripple effect. The new jobs that are created have completely different requirements regarding skills, talent, expertise and motivation than the old labour-intensive jobs that disappeared. This also creates a reserve labour force that presses labour costs down in the event of a demand for labour in the future. This class of people goes under various names such as "the working poor" (Shipler, 2005) and "the precariat" (Standing, 2014a, 2014b). Another development is that the gap between the One Per Cent class and the 99% is continually widening, thus increasing the power system of Mamounia.

The new nation we call Mamounia is thus an attempt to conceptualize globalization in a new way. What we do know is that when enterprises in the global space interact with each other and with various types of global markets, an emergent occurs, i.e. something new in the world that did not exist before. This emergent cannot be analysed by dividing it up into its constituent elements. Figuratively this would be like dissecting a bird in order to study its flight characteristics. If one divides the emergent and then attempts to put the pieces back together again into a working whole, it would be like trying to create the proud oak from the sawdust remaining on the patch where the tree was felled. Global structures cannot be analysed as if they existed under the umbrella of one or more states, precisely because it is the emergent system that should be examined. In the global economy, there are per definition no external factors, apart from the weather, the stars and the influence of the sun. The system of power in Mamounia is not influenced by anything other than its own modus operandi.

The units or elements in this power system are the global enterprises that manufacture, distribute and reintegrate following a modular logic. This modular logic consists of an extreme focus on low-costs, high quality, a high level of expertise and a high degree of innovation. This in turn reinforces the development of the global enterprises.

Although there are no institutions, constitution or laws in Mamounia, the power system in Mamounia uses the institutions and laws, such as the contract laws in the countries where Mamounia's "citizens" find the most suitable conditions (Champeil-Desplats, 2016: 159–169).

We have conceptualized Mamounia and the global power system in Figure 2.4.

Conclusion

In this chapter, we have investigated the following issue: How does globalization constitute an aspect of the fourth industrial revolution?

The answer we have arrived at can be understood along three axes. First, there is much to suggest that the exercise of power that we see in the global economy is revealing the emergence of totalitarian capitalism. This is already apparent in, for example, China and Russia. The second axis gives strength to the idea that a totalitarian form of capitalism is the consequence of the globalization of financial capital. Financial capital seems to be the backbone of totalitarian capitalism. At the same time, both financial capital and totalitarian capitalism are fostering the development of a new global "nation", which in this chapter we call Mamounia. Mamounia does not operate in accordance with geographical borders, but with symbolic borders. Mamounia also has no laws, institutions of government or constitution, unlike traditional nation states. Mamounia does however have "citizens". Most of these are the One Per Cent, who obtain information from the old continent, which consists of nation states, and who control these nation states through, among other things, financial capital.

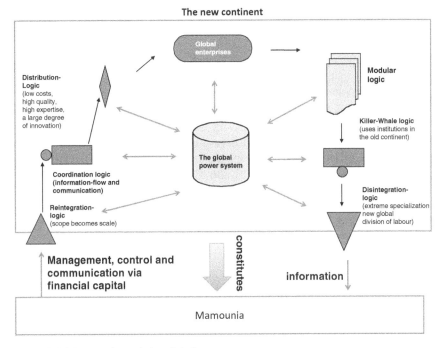

Figure 2.4 Mamounia and the global power system

Theoretical implications

When people feel they have been violated over a period of time, when Mamounia shows its claws and people become afraid of their own future and the future of their children, when their dignity is threatened and they experience a lack of respect, then they will most probably react. Their reaction may take many forms. First, there may be apathy; figuratively, this may be likened to the calm before the storm – even the birds are silent before a storm. However, like a storm, like thunder, like revenge led by the rhetoric of action, the reaction will come. Then figures representing the violated will occupy positions we have only read about from the great revolutions of the world. However, this revolution will take on completely different forms than that of the major revolutions of the past. The reaction will dress itself in new appearances, but the revolution will be similar to previous revolutions, such as the Industrial Revolution, in the sense that it will transform everything that existed before it. The reaction will probably emerge as a nostalgic yearning for the past, the security one felt before globalization and Mamounia ruled the world. The nostalgia will be felt as something good and safe, although objective analyses show that conditions before globalization were far from being safe and secure. Yet, the situation is different for many now, especially those who worked in companies that were re-located to maximize profits.

In the times we live in, the economic crises are more systemic than pre-viously, i.e., they are inter-linked. They are also systemic because many systems are connected at different levels.

This means that reactions to a crisis in one location will rapidly spread to a different location in the global economy. Since the crisis that was triggered around 2007/2008, the so-called financial crisis, the consequences have been felt around the globe. After the fall of the Berlin Wall and China's entry to the capitalist market, conditions for trade have changed. About two billion new people entered into global trade resulting in new challenges for the free market. One of these challenges is the disillusionment of many of the working and middle classes in both the US and Europe. Their anticipatory anxiety about the future has led to discontent resulting in changes in the American and European political landscapes. This dissatisfaction has led people to Nostalgia, the "yearning for the lost country".

Practical implications

The free trade and the free market economy that are embedded in neo-liberal ideology have established Mamounia as a reality. One of the results has been a redistribution of wealth from the working and middle classes in the US and Europe to the working and middle classes of China, Vietnam and India. Statis-tically, more people in the world are now better off with a global market econ-omy. Nevertheless, this statistical fact is of little consolation to the steel belt workers in the US and the working and middle classes in Wales who have lost their jobs. They have become frustrated, angry, discontented and react accord-ingly. It is an emotional revolution, not a rational one, we are witnessing. This revolution is taking place through democratic institutions. The workers' nos-talgic dream is that they want to return to their jobs in the automotive industry in Detroit, the steel industry in Michigan, the bearings industry in Illinois, the slaughterhouse industry in Denmark, and so on. But unskilled jobs will not be moved back to these regions. Another important point is that the skilled jobs will also follow, if the profits are greater where enterprises choose to re-locate.

Robots will take over in production processes to an increasing extent. Many people had hoped that this would result in jobs moving back to Europe and America, because robots do not require costly labour. In this context, it is worth noting the experience of a 31-year-old robot programmer, Michael Robinson: "I was told that although there will be increasing automation, there will always be a need for people to program robots. Yet, this is not the case as the factory has been moved to Mexico. It's hopeless!"[8] When five million factory jobs have disappeared from the US since the turn of the mil-lennium,[9] then it is understandable that people are desperate and react accordingly. The jobs are not disappearing just because the costs are lower elsewhere; they are disappearing because the profits are higher, which is something quite different. The comments of the robot programmer, Michael Robinson, show this.

Further research

On the other hand, robotization could lead to a return of factories from low-cost countries to the old industrialized nations. The rationale is that labour costs will be of less importance. Robotization will mean that US and Europe will be able to compete on productivity with countries such as China. As such, the "emotional revolution" we are seeing now will have rational positive consequences for the skilled working class.

In this scenario, three elements working together will reinforce the redistribution of wealth we have seen develop since the fall of the Berlin Wall and up until the present. The first element is the global power system. The second element is the global financial system. This system is based on a network logic where the nodes can be found in a few mega-cities such as Hong Kong, London, Frankfurt, Paris, New York, and so on. The third element is what may be termed a transition from the power of national states to globalism and Mamounia. Globalism and Mamounia are also the target of the "emotional revolution". Yet it is highly likely that the rebellion is just a ripple along the way towards increased globalism, because the strongest forces are the thinking related to a free market economy. This will only reinforce globalism and "militarize" Mamounia so that a totalitarian capitalism will spread worldwide.

The explanation for this development is simple. The free market economy with its logic of free trade will reinforce globalism. One of the consequences of the interaction between the global power system, the global financial system and globalism is that the redistribution of wealth will be reinforced. In its consequences, we will see that the rich nations become poorer because wealth creation will be moved to where the rate of profit is highest. In turn, this development will reinforce the "emotional revolution".

Political psychology seems now to be relevant in relation to globalization. People who in principle supported competition and trade now may find themselves without a job, socially declassed or threatened by both of these phenomena. In this context, one might say they are suffering the consequences of their views, or that the chickens have come home to roost.

We conclude this chapter by referring to the paradox of the philosopher Zappfe: It's what you are good at that will be your downfall; or, as in this case, capitalism is so good at competition that it will lead to its downfall.

Notes

1 In 1988 in a speech at a Communist Party conference, the Chinese President Deng Xiao Ping said that China would become rich through exports and allowing foreign capital to invest in China.
2 Arthur Schlesinger in the *Los Angeles Times*, 23 March 2003.
3 Robert Reich is Professor of Public Policy at the University of California, Berkeley. He has served in the Carter, Ford and Clinton administrations. (https://no.wikip edia.org/wiki/Robert_Reich)
4 WTO, IMF, the World Bank.
5 Financial Times, 4 February 1998, ref. in Ferguson, 2002: 279 and 468.

6   http://time.com/3890416/vestager-google-antitrust/
7   An emergent occurs if something new turns up on one level that has not previously existed on the level below. With emergent, we mean: "Let S be a system with composition A, i.e. the various components in addition to the way they are composed. If P is a property of S, P is emergent with regard to A, if and only if no components in A possess P; otherwise P is to be regarded as a resulting property with regards to A" (Bunge, 1977: 97).
8   Article in the Norwegian newspaper, *Aftenposten*, 5th December 2016.
9   *Aftenposten* 5th December 2016.

References

Bauman, Z. (2013). *Does the richness of the few benefit us all?* Polity, London.
Bonney, R. (1995). *Economic systems and state finance*, Oxford University Press, Oxford.
Bunge, M. (1977). *Treatise on basic philosophy. Vol. 3. Ontology I: The furniture of the world*, D. Reidel, Dordrecht, Holland.
Burke, J. (2004). *Al Qaeda*, I.B. Tauris, New York.
Champeil-Desplats, V. (2016). Constitutionalization outside of the state? in Robé, J.P., Lyon-Caen, A. & Vernac, S. (eds.) *Multinationals and the constitutionalization of the world power system*, Routledge, London, pp. 159–169.
Chomsky, N. (1999). *Profit over People*, Seven Stories Press, New York.
Chomsky, N. (2004). *Hegemony and Survival*, Penguin, London.
Chomsky, N. (2012). *How the World Works*, Hamish Hamilton, New York.
Chomsky, N. (2014). *Year 501: the conquest continues*, Haymarket Books, Chicago.
Chomsky, N. (2015a). *Masters of mankind*, Penguin, London.
Chomsky, N. (2015b). *The Washington connection and third world fascism*, Pluto Press, New York.
Chomsky, N. (2016). *Who rules the world*, Hamish Hamilton, London.
Cockburn, P. (2015). *The Rise of Islamic State*, Verso, London.
Dorling, D. (2015). *Inequality and the 1%*, Verso, London.
Eagleton-Pierce, M. (2016). *Neoliberalism: the key concepts*, Routledge, London.
Ferguson, N. (2002). *The cash nexus*, Penguin, London.
Freeland, C. (2013). *Plutocrats: the rise of the new superrich*, Penguin, London.
Friedman, M. (2002). *Capitalism and freedom*, University of Chicago Press, Chicago.
Gaskarth, J. (ed.). (2015). *China, India and the future of international society*, Rowman & Littlefield, London.
Giddens, A. (2002). *Runaway world: how globalization is reshaping our lives*, Profile Books, London.
Gladwell, M. (2013). *The tipping point*, Abacus, New York.
Harvey, D. (2007). *A brief history of neoliberalism*, Oxford University Press, Oxford.
Johannessen, J-A. (2016). *Innovations leads to economic crises: explaining the bubble economy*, Palgrave, London.
Kørner, M. (1995). Public credit, in Bonney, R. *Economic systems and state finance*, Oxford University Press, Oxford, pp. 507–538.
Lehmans, D.J. (2015). *Understanding trickle down economics*, Create Space, New York.
Mason, P. (2015). Foreword, in Varoufakis, Y. *The global minotaur*, Zed Books, London, pp. ix–xii.
Martell, L. (2010). *The sociology of globalization*, Polity, London.

Micklethwait, J. & Wooldridge, A. (2000). *A future perfect: the challenge and hidden promise of globalization*, Times Books, New York.

Petras, J. & Veltmeyr, H. (2011). *Beyond neoliberalism: a word to win*, Routledge, London.

Piketty, T. (2014). *Capital in the twenty-first century*, The Belknap Press of Harvard University Press, Boston.

Piketty, T. (2016). *Chronicles: on our troubled times*, Viking, London.

Raskin, M. (2015). Foreword, in Chomsky, N. *Masters of mankind*, Penguin, London, pp. 9–19.

Reich, R. (2009). *Supercapitalism*, Icon Books, New York.

Reich, R. (2015). *Saving Capitalism*, Alfred. A. Knopf, New York.

Robé, J.P. (2016). Globalization and constitutionalization of the world power system, in Robé, J.P., Lyon-Caen, A. & Vernac, S. (eds.) *Multinationals and the constitutionalization of the world power system*, Routledge, London, pp. 11–52.

Roberts, M. (2016). *The long depression*, Haymarket Books, London.

Ruggie, J.G. (2016). Foreword, in Robé, J.P., Lyon-Caen, A. & Vernac, S. (eds.) *Multinationals and the constitutionalization of the world power system*, Routledge, London, pp. xii–xvii.

Sennett, R. (1999). *The corrosion of character*, W.W. Norton, New York.

Sennett, R. (2003). *The fall of public man*, Penguin, New York.

Sennett, R. (2009). *The craftsman*, Penguin, New York.

Sennett, R. (2013). *Together*, Penguin, New York.

Shipler, D. (2005). *The working poor*, Vintage, New York.

Sowell, T. (2012). *Trickle down theory and tax cuts for the rich*, Hoover Institution Press, New York.Standing, G. (2014a). *A precariat charter*, Bloomsbury, London.

Standing, G. (2014b). *The precariat: the new dangerous class*, Bloomsbury Academic, New York.Stiglitz, P. (2002). *Globalization and its discontents*, Penguin, London.

Swider, S. (2015). *Building China, informal work and the new*, ILR Press, London.

Varoufakis, Y. (2015). *The global minotaur*, Zed Books, London.

Wacquant, L. (2007). *Urban outcast*, Polity, London.

Wacquant, L. (2009a). *Prisons of poverty*, University of Minnesota Press, New York.

Wacquant, L. (2009b). *Punishing the poor*, Duke University Press, London.

3 Robots and informats will cause economic and social crises

Introduction

In his essay *Economic Possibilities for Our Grandchildren* (1928), John Maynard Keynes predicted that by 2028, living standards in the United States and Europe would be at such a level that no one would need to think about earning money (Keynes, 1963: 358–373). The point he was trying to make was that 100 years into the future, society would have reached such an advanced level that only a few workers would be needed to keep the machines running.

In this context, the word "robot" is used to refer to a computer that is programmed to assist humans in the performance of physical and mental labour. The word robot comes from the Czech word "robota", which means "work" (Abd, 2017). The development of artificial intelligence means that robots are becoming ever more capable of performing mental labour. By informat, we mean robots with artificial intelligence which are interconnected in a global technological network. Figuratively, informats may be imagined as clusters of neurons in the human brain, which are connected to other neuron-clusters to create the various functions of human intelligence (Wilson, 2017; Winfield, 2012; Vadakkepat & Goswami, 2018). In the financial world, the use of robots by financial analysts provides an example of the use of so-called informats. Informats for use in medical surgery are already on the drawing board and will be a reality in the near future (Bleuer et al., 2017); the same applies to the use of informats in the service and education sectors (Bleuer & Bouri, 2017). Informats are understood here in the context of the above description as being emergent in relation to robots; informats can sense, analyse and reach decisions in the space of a micro-second.

In the future, if robots and informats perform most of the heavy physical labour, and mental and intellectual work, respectively, what will be left for people to do? It may be possible that people can then focus on what they do best: think, reflect and communicate. People could then use their time and resources to create a world that many only dream about today. However, this future scenario is not pre-destined. The fourth industrial revolution may easily lead to a situation where only a few profit from the new technology, while the majority will be exposed to economic and social crises. The point being made here is that it is not the robots and informats that will decide how the future unfolds; this will rather depend on what policies people adopt to deal with these technological changes.

It seems that innovation has come to represent the new economic and political "religion". All the social systems are demanding technological, economic and institutional innovations (Barrat, 2015). Of necessity, minor innovations lead to minor social and economic crises, while major innovations lead to major social and economic crises (Johannessen, 2016). In this context, Christensen uses the word "disruptions" when referring to major changes, i.e. an innovation that disrupts and makes existing business models obsolete (Christensen, 2010, 2016). Among its consequences, this leads to economic and social crises, because the old is demolished, while new ways of producing, distributing and consuming emerge.

Robotization with its innovations and disruptions will affect the way we work, employment structure and leisure time. Not least, the relationship between leisure and work will change radically, because robotization will lead to increased production (Abd, 2017).

This article examines the question: How does robotization constitute an aspect of the fourth industrial revolution?

In order to answer this question, we have formulated two research questions:

R1: How do innovation, herd behaviour and economic bubbles constitute an aspect of the fourth industrial revolution?
R2: How does destructive creation constitute an aspect of the fourth industrial revolution?

Figure 3.1 shows a representation of what is described in the introduction; it also shows how the rest of the chapter is organized.

Robots and informats: economic and social crises

Robotization will occur in parallel with social systems developing infostructure and informatization. Infostructure, as it is used here, refers to all the activities and processes that promote informatization in social systems. Miller (1978) refers to ten critical processes that exist on all system levels. These information processes are: 1) information control, 2) information channels and networks for communication, 3) information gathering, 4) information analysis, 5) information strategy, 6) information structuring and systematization, 7) information coordination, 8) information storage and retrieval, 9) information culture, and 10) distribution of information. Informatization here refers to the digitalization of the ten infostructure processes referred to above.

The robotization and informatization of society will occur through extensive expansion of the global infostructure (Brynjolfsson, & McAfee, 2014; Ford, 2016). Robots and informats will compel new ways of thinking and working, because every level of the social system will be affected (Vadakkepat &

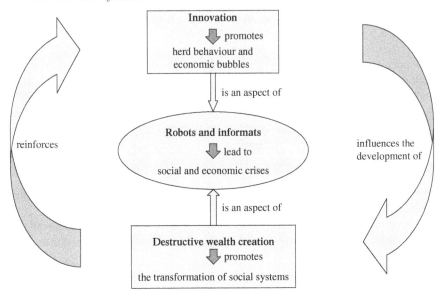

Figure 3.1 Robotization

Goswami, 2018). This will apply to economics, politics, culture and social relationships (Reich, 2015; Frankish, 2014; Gans, 2016). Keynes' essay, mentioned above, is relevant in this context; Keynes says that in such a situation, the greatest challenge people will have to face is related to the question: How will people deal with the freedom that will be created by robots and informats?[1] It is in such a situation that new ways of thinking will become central. The question "How will we live when our freedom from paid employment becomes a reality?" will be a problem for the field of philosophy. How will we spend our leisure time when we do not need to spend as much time making money to live on?

Regardless of the changes to working life brought about by the introduction of robots and informats, everyone, absolutely everyone, will be affected in one way or another (Lima, 2017; Bleuer & Bouri, 2017).

As such, Keynes was prescient in his prediction of future exponential technological development. However, in this context, a pertinent question is: Are we willing to acccpt a two-level society, in which the 1% class rule through finance capital, and the remaining 99% struggle to make ends meet (Gershuny & Fisher, 2014; Dorling, 2015)? Among the 99%, there will be major differences in terms of employment, income, leisure time and how people are employed.

What we do know with relative certainty is that the more innovations that are introduced into the market, the greater the likelihood of disruption and economic crises (Johannessen, 2016). Robots, informats, the infostructure and the informatization of society will influence how people work, their leisure time and the structure of employment. The informatization of the majority of functions will change the ways in which we work (Lima, 2017; Vadakkepat & Goswami, 2018).

One example of exploitation of informatization and the global information structure for innovative business development is the mobile photo-sharing company Instagram. When Instagram was sold to Facebook for about $1 billion, they had only 13 employees, although they had 30 million customers. On the other hand, Kodak (in a related business sector to Instagram) with 145,000 employees, went bankrupt a few months before the sale of Instagram (Reich, 2015: 206–207). The business models of the two companies were completely different. It is such a total change to business models to which Christensen refers when he uses the term disruption (Christensen, 2010, 2016). Disruption, small and large financial crises, changes in working methods and the use of informats and infostructure to produce, distribute and consume, will all inevitably lead to new ways of thinking. Instagram, Facebook, LinkedIn, and so on, are the results of new ways of thinking. Innovation has become the new economic and political religion.

In the robotized society of the future with its global information structure, if you have an idea you can then sell "the product" from your home, whether this happens to be in Wales or Detroit, to millions of potential customers without having a single employee. The ideas and access to technological expertise will, in such an economy, be the most important social mechanisms for wealth creation. In such an economy, work activities will be divided into various components; one can imagine this consisting of four components.

Firstly, there are those who have ideas and sell them in a global market. Secondly, there is the expert who is concerned with symbol analysis. This could be the financial analyst, the surgeon, the engineer, the psychologist, and so on. Thirdly, there are those who are concerned with routine work, such as the traditional industrial workers, service workers in hospitals and hotels, and bureaucrats in intermediate positions in private and public sectors. Fourthly, there is the professional group whom one could call the "front-line workers". These people are close to those they are providing service to. This includes employees working in nursing homes, home-helpers, teachers, educators, pre-school teachers and all who use their expertise to provide a service or services where physical proximity is important.

We have developed a typology of the four occupational categories that we propose will exist in the fourth industrial revolution (see Figure 3.2).

If we consider those professions under the category of "symbol analysis", such as financial analysts and surgeons, it is highly likely that the nature of their work will change when robots and informats become even more integrated in their work activities. Robots have already been introduced into the field of financial analysis, and in the future will further modify the nature of this area of work, so fewer people will be needed in this type of profession. In the relatively near future, robots and informats will also be able to perform the most complex surgical procedures (Bleuer & Bouri, 2017). Moreover,

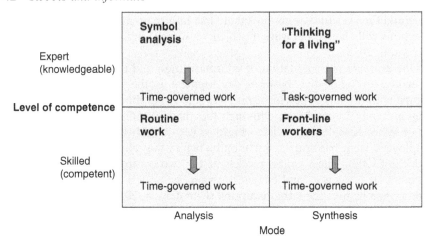

Figure 3.2 A typology of working life in the fourth industrial revolution

informatization and the infostructure will enable the interconnectedness of robots, informats and surgeons. This may result in a situation where the physical presence of the surgeon will not be needed during an operation; for instance, the surgeon may be located in Los Angeles, California, while the patient is operated on in Mehamn near the North Cape in Norway (Bleuer et al., 2017). Such a development would also totally change the way we think concerning the construction of hospitals. If robots, informats and the application of expertise at a distance become significant elements in the future treatment of patients, will the construction of giant hospital complexes still be necessary? In the future, robots, informats, the infostructure and informatization will probably result in the construction of small compact hospitals located, for instance, on street corners, like architectural gems in the centres of small towns. These small compact hospitals will most likely specialize in a particular field of medical care, and be fully equipped with up-to-date technology and robots. These small specialized robotic and informat hospitals will be staffed with service personnel with nursing educations, one or two doctors, and a robotic analysis and surgical unit. Obviously, this is far into the future, but not so far that we cannot already see such tendencies in related organization of technology (Abd, 2017; Bleuer et al., 2017; Bleuer & Bouri, 2017; Vadakkepat & Goswami, 2018).

Many of the jobs under the category of "routine work" shown in Figure 3.2 will, most probably, be moved to countries where costs are low, skills high, product quality good and where there is also a certain degree of creativity that leads to innovation (Brockbank, 2013; Bruce & Crook, 2015). On the other hand, when robots and informats take over the production of tasks under this category, it will not be necessary to move production to low-cost countries. A foretaste of this trend may be found in a report in the McKinsey Quarterly (2016), where it is stated that 78 per cent of routine physical activities in US workplaces will in the future be replaced by technological automation.[2] According to the report, the most susceptible areas of work to automation will be predictable physical work (78%), data processing (69%), data collection (64%), unpredictable physical work (25%), service work (20%), knowledge-based work (18%) and management (9%). Those workers engaged in routine work, who are unable to adjust to other types of work, will most likely become what Shipler terms "the working poor" (Shipler, 2005), or become part of the new "precariat" (Standing, 2014a, 2014b).

"Front-line workers" in the Figure 3.2 typology are all those workers in the service and healthcare sectors, including, for instance, workers in hotels, nursing homes, home helpers care, and so on. These workers will have jobs in the future, but with low income (Standing, 2014a, 2014b; Shipler, 2005; Gershuny & Fisher, 2014).

The typology also includes the category "thinking for a living" (Davenport, 2005), which will constitute knowledge workers with specialist skills (Hannah et al., 2015). These are people with highly specialized educations, at PhD level as a rule (Hanson, 2016). In all probability, this category will also consist of workers in several sub-categories, some of whom will be highly paid, while others will have middle-incomes (Ross, 2016). Most workers within this category will have work involving one or more of the twelve technological trends described by Kelly (2016) (see below). This category will involve work activities where robots and informats will play a large role. Despite the large degree of variation in the category, one common denominator will be that people will largely control their own use of time, while the workers in the other three categories of Figure 3.2 will have work that is time-governed (Lima, 2017, Hanson, 2016).

Innovation: herd behaviour and economic bubbles

One may ask: In what areas will future innovations emerge? The answer to the question can partly be found in Drucker's (1994: 44) analysis. Johannessen (2016: 153) has designed a model that provides an answer to the question. Future innovations will cause "disruptions" (Christensen, 2016), as well as small and large financial crises in the areas where productivity and quality are declining, where the real and relative costs are high, where the degree of diffusion of innovations spreads fastest, and in areas where new knowledge has the potential to become transformed into new technology. If this is correct, then it is highly likely that healthcare will be one of the major sectors in the future that will experience radical and possibly revolutionary innovations. As mentioned above, the large hospital complexes of today will probably be largely replaced by compact structures equipped with robots and informats that use the global infostructure to perform complex diagnoses and surgical procedures at low cost and of an extremely high quality.

The spirit of the times is innovation, cost control and productivity. When everyone is focused on innovation, there will be heavy investment in new opportunities by investors, and entrepreneurs will be attracted to this new area of activity. A form of "herd behaviour" will emerge in the market, figuratively speaking; i.e. resembling the behaviour of a flock of sheep or birds. This herd behaviour may easily become a problem, creating small and large bubbles in the economy. The rationale is that many will be simultaneously attracted to one or more innovations. When these economic bubbles burst, they will create minor and major economic crises, depending on the extent of the herd behaviour and how large the bubbles are. The hypothesis is that small innovations create minor economic crises, while major innovations create major economic crises (Johannessen, 2016).

One of the results of the herd behaviour will be overproduction within the area or areas that attract interest. Overproduction will lead to falling profits and bankruptcies. In this way, the system will clean itself. The next hypothesis is that the innovations that lead to the crisis will also be the same innovations that lead out of the crisis (Johannessen, 2016).

Another result of the herd behaviour is that radical innovations will lead to what Christensen (2010, 2016) terms disruption (as mentioned above). This leads to disintegration of the old business models and the emergence of new ones. Internet commerce is one such radical innovation that has destroyed old ways of doing business while simultaneously creating new businesses with completely different organizational structures. It is in this context that innovation leads to minor and major economic crises. If entire industries are transformed in a relatively short time, then people will lose their employment. Their expertise may become redundant. They lose their source of income and their futures do not look particularly bright. For some industries, this may take some time, but for others it can go quickly, very quickly. For instance, in the 1970s many of the textile workers in the OECD area were made redundant in less than one year (Hiemstra-Kupeus & Van Voss, 2010).

If it is the case as Davenport (2005: 1–11) writes that approximately half of those employed in the industrialized countries will lose their current jobs as a result of new technology, this will inevitably lead to minor and major economic and social crises. Of course, one can argue that in the longer perspective the technical evolution involving robots, nano-technology products, informats and other new technology will serve all (Abd, 2017; Wilson, 2017). In this context, one might also refer to Keynes' statement that "In the long run we are all dead". In the micro-historical perspective, the new technology will result in major upheavals for many, or, as Davenport writes, at least half of the workforce.

Since 2000, large parts of the traditional industry in the West has been moved offshore to other areas around the globe, such as China, India and other low-cost countries. In the initial developments, this concerned labour-intensive industries. Subsequently, a lot of high-tech manufacturing was also outsourced because costs were lower and profits higher. The new technology, especially that involving robots and informats, will result in many of the knowledge workers, those with higher education, losing their jobs (Ford, 2016; Beaudry et al., 2013). Many knowledge workers will become socially declassed and have to settle for jobs with lower salaries, greater uncertainty and poor expectations regarding future prospects (Bauman, 2013; Wacquant, 2009a, 2009b; Barrat, 2015).

The fact that the two expressions "the working poor" (Shipler, 2005) and "the precariat" (Standing, 2014a, 2014b) are gaining more attention perhaps reflects the situation that the outlook for many is very poor. Amongst the knowledge workers, the following occupational groups: journalists, lawyers, financial analysts, doctors, marketers, people in the advertising industry, etc. will experience that their jobs will be threatened by robots, informats, informatization and artificial intelligence (Brynjolfsson & McAfee, 2014; Gans, 2016). Moreover, all the routine-based and repetitive tasks, both in manufacturing and service-oriented professions, will also be threatened (Lima, 2017; Gershuny & Fisher, 2014).

While the industrial revolution increased agricultural productivity, the knowledge revolution increases the productivity of all types of knowledge workers (Drucker, 1999a, 1999b). The long view is that workers first migrated from agriculture to industry, and now from industry to knowledge occupations (Hannah et al., 2015; Hanson, 2016). While automation was industrialization's driving force, informatization is the driving force behind the knowledge-revolution. Informatization and informats are increasingly driven by cognitive robots based on artificial intelligence and interconnected through global technological networks (Wilson, 2017; Abd, 2017; Lima, 2017). As an extension of this, we see the emergence of cognitive technologies (Davenport, 2005: 4). Cognitive technologies may be understood as computers that observe, analyse, uncover patterns, create syntheses and make decisions (Ross, 2016; Wilson, 2017; Abd, 2017). For instance, your doctor, through instant access to cognitive robots and informats, may acquire knowledge that only the most skilled doctors in the world possessed previously (Davenport & Kirby, 2005: 4–5). This will apply in the near future also to car-driving, airline operations, financial analysis, legal evaluations, surgery, medical and psychological diagnoses, etc.

Cognitive technologies will enable professions to access the foremost global expertise in their fields through interconnected robots and informats that will create an open window of global knowledge. This knowledge window will obviously not be free, but will result in new competences and professions emerging. The resulting innovations will after a time-leg result in a situation where entrepreneurs and others flock to invest (Sassen, 2002; Sennett, 2013). This will result in herd behaviour encouraging the growth of an economic bubble, which when it bursts after a period will have consequences for individuals and social systems (Johannessen, 2016).

We have visualized this development in Figure 3.3.

The human brain will come into competition with artificial intelligence, because around 2026 robots will have the same processing capacity as humans (Lima, 2017; Abd, 2017). This means that all the work that is based on analysis and pattern recognition of large amounts of data will be able to be performed

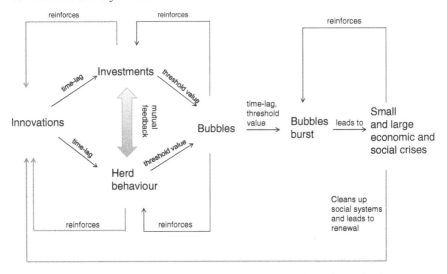

Figure 3.3 Herd behaviour, economic bubbles and economic and social crises

better by cognitive robots and informats than by humans (Wilson, 2017; Srinivasa, 2017).

In the short term, future innovations will disrupt the market leading to high levels of unemployment, and economic and social crises. However, as mentioned above, the same innovations that led to the crisis will, after a time-lag, also lead the way out of the crisis creating economic growth and rising prosperity for most people (Susskind & Susskind, 2015; Winfield, 2012). In the future, robots, informats and people will most probably work side by side; however, this will not be the case in the short term, because herd behaviour and economic bubbles will result in changes to the economy and social system that will lead to counter reactions against the new (Wood, 2016; Zuboff, 2017; Varoufakis, 2015). This also occurred during industrialization's childhood, when workers destroyed the machines because in many cases they replaced artisans and farm workers, making them redundant. At the beginning of the fourth industrial revolution, we can witness a similar reaction with the rising sentiment that "everything was so much better in the past". This may be understood as a nostalgia-reaction, which can have various economic, social and especially political consequences. For instance, Brexit, Trumpism and the emergence of national-conservative parties in Europe may be considered as elements of this "nostalgia" reaction.

Robots and informats will be the knowledge workers' future partners not competitors (Barrat, 2015). Just as the car was a mechanism that enabled geographic freedom, the robots and informats, and the new cognitive computers, will function as helpers enabling cognitive freedom (Bleuer et al., 2017). Robots and informats will initially outcompete some groups of knowledge workers (Bruce & Crook, 2015). In the mid-term and slightly longer term, the robots, robotization, informats and informatization will enhance our ability to increase productivity and quality, and result in new and more exciting work (Brynjolfsson & McAfee, 2014). Innovations may destroy established structures, but they also create long-term preconditions for economic growth.

Machines introduced into the English textile industry threatened the liveli-hoods of textile workers and weavers. Many of these workers banded together calling themselves Luddites;[3] with the aim of protecting their own jobs, they set about destroying the machines. The Luddites included workers in textile workshops, but also self-employed weavers in the cottage industry (Henty, 2016). The textile machines were an innovation in the industry, but also represented a "crisis" for those who lost their jobs, i.e. factory workers and cottage-workers. Their traditional skills were made redundant, and they lost their income. However, in the medium term, productivity of mills increased and new workers were hired into the industry, but with other functions than the traditional textile workers. Thus, in the short term, innovations led to personal and social crises; in the medium term, the innovations created more jobs than they destroyed; while in the long term, the innovations created economic growth and prosperity for most people (Jones, 2006).

Just as there was a struggle against the introduction of textile machines, we have also witnessed a struggle against automation (Jones, 2006: 20–35). Based on this historical knowledge, it should not surprise anyone if a similar struggle was initiated against robots, informats and informatization. Robotics and informatization will affect service jobs, knowledge workers' jobs and the administrative layers in organizations. In other words, these are what one may call "middle class" jobs. Therefore, it is highly probable that the middle class will be affected by these developments and become socially declassed in the fourth industrial revolution; robotization and informatization may even con-tribute to a dissolution of the middle class (Davidow & Malone, 2014). It is understandable that people are worried that robots and informats will take over their jobs. In this situation, it is the knowledge workers who have the most to fear (Brynjolfson & McAfee, 2014). Studies conducted in the United States show that the demand for knowledge workers reached its peak around the year 2000 (Beaudry et al., 2013). Concurrent with these developments, universities worldwide are spewing out yet more graduates qualified to work in the knowledge sector. Following the laws of economics, price is always a function of supply and demand, and consequently, knowledge workers' wages will fall in the future. The inequality between wages in various sectors will therefore increase (Piketty, 2014, 2016). Managers, financial analysts, investment funds analysts, investment bank employees, and so on, will be the salary winners (Spraque, 2015; Susskind & Susskind, 2015). The majority of knowledge workers will be salary losers (Davenport & Kirby, 2005: 6–7). Such developments indicate that extreme specialization will be the way to go to secure rewards. In the future, employees with regular university qualifica-tions within the fields of law, medicine, engineering, economics and business administration will not receive particularly high salaries (Davidow & Malone, 2014). This means that robotization and informatization will create a new "working class" who will consist of knowledge workers with extensive education and relatively low salaries, and service workers with little education and low salaries. These developments will also be accompanied by the emergence of the so-called "precariat" (Standing, 2014a, 2014b) and "the working poor" (Shipler, 2005).

The "new working class" is characterized by a growing discontent. This dissatisfaction shows itself in many ways. In the US, Trumpism may be considered one "symptom" of these new developments. In Europe, Brexit and the emergence of national-conservative movements may be partly explained by various types of discontent. We are witnessing a rational dissatisfaction in relation to future prospects, an emotional dissatisfaction and political discontent. The political discontent affects the established politicians who are unable to provide answers to the problems and the challenges people are experiencing. The emotional dissatisfaction is related to the social declassification of some groups, and the fear of what the future may bring for people and their children. The rational discontent concerning future prospects may be linked to the idea that education should be worthwhile and lead to well-paying jobs. However, more and more people see that this is not the case. Master's degrees in fields such as psychology, medicine, law and other fields are perhaps not enough to provide meaningful, well-paid jobs; today, the job market often requires that graduates need to use a further five to ten years to specialize (Bruce & Crook, 2015; Gershuny & Fisher, 2014).

Destructive wealth creation: transformation of social systems

Innovation is the lifeblood of the modern economy, say Dyer et al. (2010: 1). The metaphor may be elaborated on by saying that some of this lifeblood leads to "bad blood" between people, because innovation leads to changes, and in some contexts transforms large parts of the economy, so that more people will experience social crises. Radical innovations transform whole wealth creation chains, and affect many people's lives (Christensen, 2010; 2016). After a time-lag, radical innovations create the new. Before the new is created, the old is destroyed. This is what is meant here by destructive wealth creation. While something is destructed, the new grows out of this destruction, like the phoenix bird rising from its own ashes. It is in such a context that Schumpeter (1951, 1954, 1989) uses the term creative destruction to describe what happens when innovations enter the market. Schumpeter makes the point that the creative upswing is related to the destruction caused by innovations. In other words, Schumpeter's concept creative destruction relates to a long-term perspective. Thus, innovations may be considered to have destructive and wealth creation elements. In the short term, the old is destroyed, while in the long term, the new is created. Destructive wealth creation relates to the short term, when economic bubbles develop and when they burst. Creative destruction relates to the upturn when the new is created and the old has been destroyed.

In the short term, innovations lead to bad blood between people, because they lead to new business models, while others are forced into bankruptcy; many people lose their jobs, some lose their income, and some people and families also experience social crises as a result of innovations. In the longer term, most people will benefit. However, this does not help matters in the short term for those who experience the worst consequences of small and large innovations. Those who are affected negatively by destructive wealth creation risk being degraded to a lower social class, while others are lying "wounded on the ground" and are in need of a blood transfusion from the lifeblood Dyer et al. (2011: 1) speak of. In such a situation, policies are needed to mitigate the most harmful effects of destructive wealth creation.

There are many historical examples of destructive wealth creation. The internal combustion engine replaced the steam engine; motor-driven ships replaced sailing ships, the refrigeration industry replaced other methods of keeping food fresh, such as salting; cars replaced horse-driven carriages, and so on. The social consequences of the above developments were in many cases considerable; some local communities were desolated, while others flourished and new ones joined and grew into large cities. Some businesses went bankrupt while others were started-up and prospered.

In recent times, we have examples of businesses that failed or ran into difficulties because they did not make the transition during changing times: for instance, Facit AB, the Swedish manufacturer of mechanical calculators who failed to make the transition to digital calculators; Kodak who did not see the new opportunities created by the infostructure and thus went bankrupt (Instagram took over many of Kodak's functional areas); Nokia who were unable to compete with the new smartphones that hit the market is another example (Skype now offers free telephone services); and Apple's iPad that outcompeted Sony Walkman, and so on.

Innovations create gaps in the market so the market is knocked out of balance. The greater the innovation, the larger will be the gaps, and, consequently, the greater will be the imbalance that occurs in the market. Entrepreneurs flock to exploit this gap in the market which creates opportunities for super-profits. The more entrepreneurs who try to fill the gap, the faster the rate of profit will fall, because competition forces prices down. After some time over-investment will occur due to this "herd behaviour". Economic bubbles are created, small and large. If there is no intervention at an overarching policy level the bubbles will burst, with the consequences this has for individuals, families, organizations and nations (Johannessen, 2016).

Destructive wealth creation changes the ground rules for entire industries, such as Amazon who changed the market of the book industry, and Create-Space which made online publishing possible without editors as gatekeepers and intermediaries. Dell created an online model for direct sales of computing solutions; Rent the Runway offers for hire tailor-made designer pieces;

Research in Motion developed the "BlackBerry"; EBay developed online auctions between consumers and sellers; PayPal developed safe payment solutions over the Internet; Netflix, ViaPlay, etc. offer online movies; Uber established a global taxi business without owning a single taxi; Facebook have become the world's most popular news media without creating any of the news content; Airbnb do not own a single property, but have become a leading global provider of accommodation. All these companies have emerged as a result of the new technology and have created solutions that have led to large and small destructions of many established businesses and to economic and social crises; but they have also created wealth for new businesses.

One new aspect of the fourth industrial revolution will be that products will be transformed into services and processes (Kelly, 2016: 6–7). The "product" as we know it will be developed into a robot or informat that constantly updates information about our habits, desires and needs. Informats will be equipped with flexible technology that continuously adapts to user complexity. Consider a product such as a shoe. The shoe may be developed into a service product in the form of an informat that adapts to the user. For instance, consider a user with slightly different leg lengths after a hip replacement; the informat/shoe will be able to compensate for this. The shoe will also expand in the heat, become a winter shoe in the winter and a summer shoe in the summer, and so on. In other words, the shoe will become a service unit rather than a product (Kelly, 2016: 7). Products will be able to evolve into service units due to complex information processing (Case, 2016). These information processes will be connected to the individual service units, such as a shoe. The shoe will be connected to a global information system. If the user limps this will be rectified. If the user gets tired, the shoe will change shape. If the user develops an incipient disease, the shoe, and other service units the user uses, will have access to medical records, notify the appropriate entities, undertake measures and make corrections so the body is able to adapt and regain health balance. The ethical implications of such technology will be continuously discussed. If the individual does not want to be part of such a complex information system, he/she can disengage themselves from the information system.

Creativity is nothing new. However, what is new is that it will be the most sought after talent in the future (Dyer et al., 2010: 1). The reasoning is simple. Global competition entails competing on cost, quality and expertise, as well as innovation. Innovation provides the greatest profits, because the new can be priced higher than the monopoly price for a period. Innovation requires creativity. Therefore creativity will be the most sought after managerial skill in the future (Dyer et al., 2010: 261, note 1).

Change has become the new stability. Creativity is the new core competence. Just as you have finance departments in organizations that manage economic processes, in the future, creativity departments will most probably be established to manage creative processes. The reasoning is simple:

innovation is the area businesses will be able to stand out in the global economy, and creativity is a prerequisite of innovation.

The individual or business that is unable to adapt to changes will be made redundant. These changes will involve technology in one way or another. Technological changes transform established systems, creating new organizational structures and management roles (Brynjolfsson & McAfee, 2014; Brynjolfsson & Saunders, 2013). These technological changes, which will be connected to complex information systems, will be present everywhere. They will be in our computers, cars, clothes, shoes, pens, telephones, watches, jewellery, and so on. The information will be interconnected with global networks, where intelligence exists in interconnected structures of information networks (Catmull, 2014; Coates & Morrison, 2016). Which technological trends can we identify that will affect our future in the next thirty years? Kelly (2016) has a clear answer to this question, and proposes twelve technological trends that will be an integral part of our lives. We base the following trends on Kelly's description, but have created a different synthesis.

1 Technology of maintenance

Explanation: Everything changes over time (ref. The second law of thermodynamics).

2 Cognifying technology

Explanation: Smart freely available solutions will be developed based on artificial intelligence, robotics and informats that solve problems that we previously perceived as complex and intractable.

3 Technology of memory

Explanation: Everything that reaches the Internet is being copied, stored, retrieved, modified, re-copied and re-stored.

4 Screen technology

Explanation: Interaction via the written word in the book is replaced by interaction via various types of screens.

5 Loan and rent technology

Explanation: The trend is a shift from product to service, i.e. a technology that creates access without the need to own, such as Uber, Airbnb, Netflix, Photoshop, etc. Any product where customers have to wait, or costs are high, they develop their own "Uber for X", i.e. freelancers that can fill your needs.

6 Sharing technology

Explanation: The technology is free for all to use without charge, such as Skype, Wikipedia, etc. The trend is a wiki for everything, Creative Commons, Pinterest, Digg, Reddit, Tumblr, etc. This is a form of digital socialism where one can freely share what one has, so everyone can access it. Sharing technology is extremely decentralized. In the future, this technology will enable sharing opportunities in areas we are unaware of today, or we do not value.

7 Filtering and summarization technology

There is a constant barrage of new things, such as songs, books, blogs, online postings, and so on, so that it is impossible for both the man-in-the-street and specialists to keep up to date. Consequently, filtration and summarization technology is in demand to personalize and anticipate desires. Marketing based on people's searches on the Internet, for instance, Amazon, Google Books, Google Scholar, etc. You can also imagine a cognitive avatar that exists online, where your online searches are categorized and filtered to anticipate your desires; personalized products and services are then tested by the avatar before being sent to you.

8 Remixing technology

Explanation: When existing products are linked together and recombined entirely new solutions will arise that meet both old needs and new desires that have not yet been realized. Connecting established solutions will result in economic growth. For instance, consider, Snapchat, Flickr, WhatsApp, 3-D printers, and so on.

9 Synthetic technology

Explanation: This technology makes the experience more real than reality. For instance, holographic projections, avatars that are designed in solid material, a form of artificial world where dreams, needs and desires can be played out.

10 Personal diagnostic technology

Explanation: Watches and clothes that perform various health measurements, such as measuring your pulse, blood pressure, blood sugar level; or analysing your blood after consumption of food and beverages displayed on a screen so the individual understands how various types of food and liquids affect his/ her body. This will give us better insight into how our health is affected by consumption and habits and give us the opportunity to change our behaviour. This technology may also be able to send signals directly to a robot or informat that decides courses of action. This technology will improve and be more accessible, and have a single focus: your health.

11 Mass editing technology

Explanation: Wikipedia was theoretically impossible, but practically tolerant of errors. Even the Supreme Court in the US have referred to Wikipedia articles. Everyone has the opportunity of developing and changing something in this type of wiki technology. One can imagine a situation where laws and regulations, diagnoses and medication may be developed in the same way: impossible in theory, but possible in practice. Everything that is now done by experts may be done in the future by a wiki tool that has been developed and edited by everyone and anyone, without exception.

12 Interactive technology

Explanation: Development of a "super-mind" on the planet Tellus that thinks and decides what is best for the whole and gives instructions to members (nations, institutions and businesses). This could conceivably be a materialization of the Gaia hypothesis, but now created by people. Such an interactive technology will be able to regulate the complex relationships that exist to preserve and maintain Tellus as a habitable planet where the whole and the parts are interconnected.

Our synthesis of the twelve technology trends are visualized in Figure 3.4.

Conclusion

The problem for discussion in this chapter was: How does robotization constitute an aspect of the fourth industrial revolution?

Robotization will lead to herd behaviour in the market and the growth of economic bubbles. After a given period, these minor and major economic bubbles will burst leading to minor and major economic, social and political

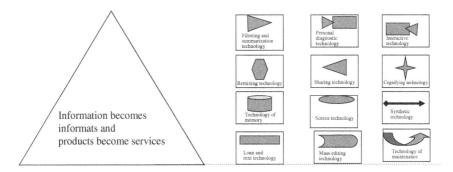

Figure 3.4 Technological trends that will create our future up until 2050

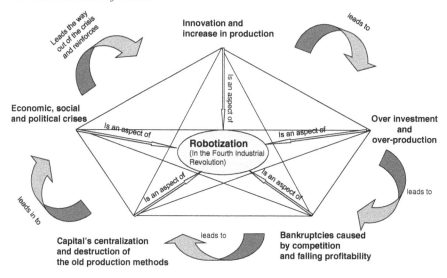

Figure 3.5 Robotization and the fourth industrial revolution

crises, and transformation of our social systems. However, the innovation that brings about a crisis will also be the innovation that shows us the way out of it. The time that elapses between the crisis and the upturn will be used to put things in order: to get rid of the old and bring in the new. This period is referred to as a crisis, but could just as well be packaged as a period of refurbishment to remove economic "tumours" and then start over with an economically healthy "body", cleansed of old dross. When using such a metaphor in an economic context, one should be aware that despite the long-term improvement of the economy's health, in a human context, many people, families and social systems will be adversely affected in the process.

We have developed an analytical model that visualizes the answer to the question posed in this chapter (Figure 3.5).

Notes

1 Of course, Keynes did not use the words robots and informats, but described a future where machines and automats perform most of the jobs done today by people.
2 Report in McKinsey Quarterly: "Where machines could replace humans–and where they can't … yet" (the Norwegian newspaper, *Aftenposten*, 3 January 2017).
3 "Luddites" were early 19th century English textile workers who destroyed machines; they were named after Ned Ludd, famed for having broken textile machines in a fit of rage. The Luddite Movement started in Nottingham and culminated in a region-wide rebellion that lasted from 1811 to 1816. The Movement was opposed by employers and eventually brutally suppressed with military force. The term Neo-Luddism means one opposed to new technologies in general (Henty, 2016).

References

Abd, K.K. (2017). *Intelligent scheduling of robotic flexible assembly cells*, Springer, London.

Barrat, J. (2015). *Our final invention*, St Martin's Griffin, London.

Bauman, Z. (2013). *Does the richness of the few benefit us all?* Polity, London.

Beaudry, P., Green, D.A. & Sand, B. (2013). *The great reversal in the demand for skill and cognitive tasks*, National Bureau of Economic Research, WP., no. 18901, New York.

Bleuer, H. & Bouri, M. (2017). *New trends in medical and service robots: assistive, surgical and educational robotics*, Springer, London.

Bleuer, H., Bouri, M. & Mandada, F.C. (2017). *New trends in medical and service robots*, Springer, London.

Brockbank, W. (2013). *Overview and logic*, in Ulrich, D., Brockbank, W., Younger, J. & Ulrich, M. (eds.), *Global HR competencies: mastering competitive value from the outside in*, McGraw Hill, New York, pp. 3–27.

Bruce, D. & Crook, G. (2015). *The dream café: lessons in the art of radical innovation*, John Wiley & Sons, New York.

Brynjolfsson, E. & McAfee, A. (2014). *The second machine age*, W.W. Norton & Company, New York.

Brynjolfsson, E. & Saunders, A. (2013). *Wired for innovation: how information technology is reshaping the economy*, The MIT Press, London.

Case, S. (2016). *The third wave*, Simon & Schuster, New York.

Catmull, E. (2014). *Creativity Inc.*, Bantam Books, New York.

Christensen, C.M. (2010). *disrupting class, expanded edition: how disruptive innovation will change the way the world learns*, McGraw-Hill, New York.

Christensen, C.M. (2016). *The Clayton M. Christensen reader*, Harvard Business School Press, Boston.

Coates, K.S. & Morrison, B. (2016). *Dream factories*, Dundum, London.

Davenport, T. H. (2005). *thinking for a living, how to get better performance and results from knowledge workers*, Harvard Business School Press, Boston.

Davenport, T.H. & Kirby, J. (2005). *Only human need apply: winners and losers in the age of the smart machines*, Harper Business, New York.

Davidow, W.H. & Malone, M.C. (2014). What happens to society when robots replace workers? *Harvard Business Review*, 10 December.

Drucker, P.F. (1994). *The age of discontinuity*, Transaction Publishers, New York.

Drucker, P.F. (1999a). Knowledge worker productivity: the biggest challenge, *California Management Review*, 41, 2: 79–94.

Drucker. P.F. (1999b). *Management challenges for the 21st century*, Harper Collins, New York.

Dyer, J., Gregersen, H. & Christensen, C.M. (2010). *The innovator's DNA: mastering the five skills of disruptive innovators*, Harvard Business Review Press, Boston.

Ford, M. (2016). *The rise of the robots: technology and the threat of mass unemployment*, One World, London.

Frankish, K. (2014). *The Cambridge handbook of artificial intelligence*, Cambridge University Press, Cambridge.

Gans, J. (2016). *The disruption dilemma*, The MIT Press, Boston.

Gershuny, J. & Fisher, K. (2014). *Post-industrious society: why work time will not disappear for our grandchildren*, Center for Time Use Research, Department of Sociology, University of Oxford, Oxford.

Hannah, E., Scott, J. & Trommer, S. (2015). *Expert knowledge in global trade*, Routledge, London.

Hanson, R. (2016). *The age of Em: work, love and life when robots rule the world*, Oxford University Press, Oxford.

Henty, G.A. (2016). *Through the fray: a tale of the Luddite Riot*, Create Space, New York.

Hiemstra-Kuperus, E. & Van Voss, L.H. (2010). *The Ashgate companion to the history of textile workers 1650–2000*, Routledge, London.

Johannessen, J-A. (2016). *Innovation leads to economic crises: explaining the bubble economy*, Palgrave, London.

Jones, S. (2006). *Against technology: from Luddites to Neo-Luddism*, CRC Press, New York.

Kelly, K. (2016). *The inevitable: understanding the 12 technological forces that will shape our future*, Viking, New York.

Keynes, J.M. (1963). *Essays in persuasion*, WW. Norton, New York.

Lima, P.U. (2017). *Autonomous mobile robotics: a system perspective*, CRS Press, New York.

Miller, J.G. (1978). *Living systems*, McGraw-Hill, New York.

Piketty, T. (2014). *Capital in the twenty-first century*, The Belknap Press of Harvard University Press, Boston.

Piketty, T. (2016). *Chronicles: On our troubled times*, Viking, London

Reich, R. (2015). *Saving capitalism: for the many, not the few*, Alfred A. Knopf, New York.

Ross, A. (2016). *The industries of the future*, Simon & Schuster, London.

Sassen, S. (2002). *Global networks/linked cities*, Routledge, New York.

Schumpeter, J. (1951) *Theory of economic development*, Harvard University Press, Boston.

Schumpeter, J. (1954). *History of economic analysis*, Oxford University Press, Oxford.

Schumpeter, J. (1989). *Business cycles*, Porcupine Press, New York.

Sennett, R. (2013). *Together*, Penguin, New York.

Shipler, D. (2005). *The working poor*, Vintage, New York.

Spraque,S. (2015). What can labor productivity tell us about the US economy, *US Bureau of Labor Statistics, Beyond the numbers* 3, 12 (May).

Srinivasa, R. (2017). *Whose global village: rethinking how technology shapes the world*, NYU Press, London.

Standing, G. (2014a). *A precariat charter*, Bloomsbury, London.

Standing, G. (2014b). *The precariat: the new dangerous class*, Bloomsbury Academic, New York.Susskind, R. & Susskind, D. (2015). *The future of professions: how technology will transform the work of human experts*, OUP, Oxford.

Vadakkepat, P. & Goswami P. (eds.). (2018). *Humanoid robotics: a reference*, Springer, London.

Varoufakis, Y. (2015). *The global minotaur*, Zcd Books, London.

Wacquant, L. (2009a). *Punishing the poor*, Duke University Press, London.

Wacquant, L. (2009b). *Prisons of poverty*, University of Minnesota Press, New York.

Wilson, M. (2017). *Implementation of robot systems*, Butterworth-Heinemann, New York.

Winfield, A. (2012). *Robotics*, Oxford University Press, Oxford.

Wood, E.M. (2016). *Democracy against capitalism*, Verso, London.

Zuboff, S. (2017). *Master or slave: the fight for the soul of our information civilization*, Public Affairs, New York.

4 Aspects of a policy architecture for the fourth industrial revolution

Introduction

The fourth industrial revolution is the result of increased education, new technology, globalization of the economy, politics, culture and human relations (Schwab, 2016; Abd, 2017).

To investigate policy implications in the fourth industrial revolution, we have chosen an approach where we examine the following four subsystems (Bunge, 1998):

- The economic subsystem, focusing on material and technological resources.
- The political subsystem, focusing on power and distribution of resources.
- The collaborative subsystem, focusing on relationships and networks.
- The cultural subsystem, focusing on values and norms.

There is much to suggest that the rationality of the economic subsystem, i. e. the ideas and thinking concerning economic and technological issues, has impacted the cultural subsystem, the political subsystem and the relationships between people (Dorling, 2015; Chomsky, 2016a; Case, 2016).

The present management structure, as we know it, has been largely developed in relation to industrialization. However, when industrial workers become technicians who control robots and informats[1] a new type of management will emerge. This will also occur in traditional industrial companies (Brynjolfsson & McAfee, 2014).

The industrial society is associated with values and norms other than those prevailing at the start of the fourth industrial revolution (Castells, 2009; Chomsky, 2012). Central to the industrial society was the growth of trade unions and the focus on workers' rights. Additionally, the concept of fairness was a central value: this was understood to equate with the fair distribution of material resources, equal access to cultural institutions, equal participation in political life and strong resistance to the master–servant distinction in every sense (Dickinson, 2016; McGill, 2016).

At the beginning of the fourth industrial revolution, a major challenge is to incorporate in collective solutions respect and responsibility for, and the dignity of, the individual (Piketty, 2016; Roat, 2016). Another challenge will be to integrate productive capital and knowledge capital, while balancing financial capital so that it promotes sustainable value creation and does not operate within short time horizons which may damage knowledge-building in society as a whole (Rodrik, 2011; Rojecki, 2016).

While the prevailing normative basis in the industrial society was to ensure social and collective solutions, there is much to suggest that the normative basis at the start of the fourth industrial revolution will largely be concerned with ensuring individual solutions (Rosa & Mathys-Treio, 2015).

Globalization is not a result of democratic processes in the political sub-system. It may be better understood as an emergent dimension that has grown through interactions between the economic, political, cultural and collaborative subsystems. In the industrial epoch, it was largely the political subsystem that governed and controlled activities in the economic subsystem. However, at the beginning of the knowledge society and the fourth industrial revolution, characterized by globalization, the governing instruments of the national state's political subsystem do not have the same impact (Sennett, 2003).

At the organizational level, this development has led to a high focus on costs in order to remain globally competitive. In practice, this has led to global businesses and companies avoiding domestic taxation by using tax havens (Beck, 1992: 19; McGill, 2016). Consequently, if this development continues and increases the social contract between businesses, employees and nations may be worsened (Beck, 2015).

If the funding of collective resources is unevenly distributed in favour of businesses and capital income, this will probably increase social conflicts at the national level. This may reinforce the idea of "us against them" – thus encouraging a scapegoat mentality (Bauman, 2013). In its consequences, this may lead to the loosening of social ties in the nation state. Consequently, globalization may result in the loosening of social ties between businesses, workers and the national state. In addition, the idea of loyalty between businesses and employees may become less important. The labour market may also become more flexible of necessity, where workers will be expected to be available depending on the needs of employers. This "flexibility" will greatly reduce established working conditions. If globalization manifests itself in this way, this will probably result in new forms of collaboration and new collaborative networks that we can only guess the consequences of. If such a development takes anchor, there will be a loosening of social ties and a process of social disintegration will slowly develop. In turn, this will reinforce the trend of individualization that we can already see the contours of today in the competitive global economy (Sennett, 2003, 2013; Bauman, 2013).

The following developments may occur: global businesses will push down costs and increase profits. National budgets will be put under pressure because of a reduction in national income, while there will be an increasing demand for welfare services to be maintained or improved. Thus, although global businesses will make greater profits there will be increased pressure on social welfare systems, probably resulting in an even greater difference between the rich and poor (Mason, 2015; McGill, 2016).

In this introduction, we have attempted to describe the following research problem: the fourth industrial revolution may develop in such a way that it may be detrimental to organizations and nations.

To address this research problem, we have formulated the following main research question: Which overall policy can be developed so that the fourth industrial revolution will lead to greater value creation for the benefit of an increasing number of people?

In order to answer this research question we have formulated the following four sub-research questions:

Sub-research question 1: Which policy can be developed for the economic subsystem so that the fourth industrial revolution will lead to greater value creation for the benefit of an increasing number of people?

Sub-research question 2: Which policy can be developed for the political subsystem so that the fourth industrial revolution will lead to greater value creation for the benefit of an increasing number of people?

Sub-research question 3: Which policy can be developed for the cultural subsystem so that the fourth industrial revolution will lead to greater value creation for the benefit of an increasing number of people?

Sub-research question 4: Which policy can be developed for the collaborative system so that the fourth industrial revolution will lead to greater value creation for the benefit of an increasing number of people?

We have summarized the introduction in Figure 4.1, which also shows how the rest of the chapter is organized.

The economic subsystem

In this section we investigate the question: Which policy can be developed for the economic subsystem so that the fourth industrial revolution will lead to greater value creation for the benefit of an increasing number of people?

In the following, six elements will be discussed as aspects of a policy for the economic subsystem in the fourth industrial revolution. The six elements are: democratization of the economic subsystem, economic equalization, control over one's daily life, directing competition policy, the organized market and unique competence.

Democratization of the economic subsystem

Democratization of economic activity is important because this will increase engagement and motivation, thus promoting value creation (Charnock & Starosta, 2016). On the other hand, if financial capital is given free rein this

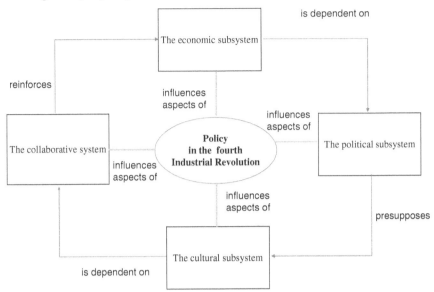

Figure 4.1 A policy architecture for the fourth industrial revolution

will result in a centralization of power and capital in the hands of the few (McGill, 2016; Bauman, 2013).

Directed competition policy and an organized market will be able to function as balancing mechanisms. Through these social mechanisms, engagement and motivation will promote value creation, while competition will function as a driving force for increased prosperity (Sennett, 2013; Rosa & Mathys-Treio, 2015). However, without these balancing mechanisms financial capital and uncontrolled competition could result in tearing the system apart (Bauman, 2013; Beck, 2015). Such a development would probably lead to a new type of capitalism emerging, namely feudal capitalism. Consequently, like Zappfe's paradox,[2] unrestrained competition will probably result in the self-destruction of the system.

Economic equalization and control over one's daily life

The purpose of economic equalization is to both ensure the welfare of the individual and to provide the basis for the social contract (Piketty, 2014: 1–33). If the social contract is eroded, the basis for social systems will also slowly disappear, paving the way for destructive individualism (Sennett, 2003; Roat, 2016).

Regarding economic equalization, output control is of interest because it focuses attention on the desired results (Hills et al., 2009). A focus on results should also be the position emphasized on all levels in the economic system, because it promotes responsibility, participation and greater control over one's daily life (Reich, 2015; Antonelli, 2001).

Setting standards for what is desirable at various levels promotes people's control over their own daily lives in relation to the economic processes they participate in (Charnock & Starosta, 2016).

Output control is particularly important in the knowledge economy because it stimulates participation and commitment (Dickinson, 2016). Output control as it is used here refers to having control of the results and what is delivered. However, output control must not be confused with goal management, which is something quite different. Output control is analogous with Wassily Leontief's Input-Output Model,[3] Stafford Beer's Theory of Living Systems (Beer, 1979, 1981, 1995) and Drucker's discussion of what motivates knowledge workers (Drucker, 1999a, 1999b). Knowledge workers differ from industrial workers regarding this point, i.e. having the possibility of controlling their own daily life (Gans, 2016; Gollan, 2010). This refers to control over your own use of time: not what you have to do, just where and when to do it. It is easier for the knowledge worker when the emphasis is on output control rather than process control (Bennis et al., 2012; Biswas-Diener, 2011; Boxall & Purcell, 2010).

It is always important to focus on the balance between stability and change, change and conservation, order and chaos, regulation and market, security and risk, because this balance helps to ensure economic equalization (Castelfranchi, 2007; Davies, 2003: 231–240). However, this requires an active government that focuses on the above, and responsible citizens who can help facilitate change and innovation processes (Harrison & Freeman, 2004; Lele, 2011).

An active focus on the three elements – the democratization of economic life, economic equalization and control over one's daily life – will counterbalance one of the greatest financial consequences of globalization: namely, the centralization of financial capital (Harvey, 2007; Mason, 2015). The centralization of financial capital is characterized by acquisitions, mergers, mergers of both finance centres and centres for managing real capital (Avent, 2016; Bolanski & Chiapello, 2017).

Economies of scale are viewed as having benefits such as cost saving and the concentration of power; however, the disadvantages are the social and economic consequences (Chomsky, 2016a, 2016b).

Directing competition and the organized market

If hyper-competition is the fundamental regulatory principle of economic life, this will probably lead to the emergence of a raw and brutal capitalism (Gupta et al., 2016; Harvey, 2007). Instead of such hyper-competition, which has been advocated by the neoliberalists since the 1980s, it is possible to imagine a policy of directed competition and an organized market (Petras et al., 2013; Avent, 2016). Directed competition balances the various negative factors in the so-called free market where hyper-competition prevails (Petras & Veltmeyr, 2011; Banki, 2015). Directed competition requires framework conditions that are relatively durable. Possibly, the most important framework conditions in directed competition are the collective agreements, laws and regulations that regulate the relationships and consequences of economic activities (Bolanski & Chiapello, 2017).

In directed competition the idea is that the market must be tamed, just as a wild horse needs to be tamed. When a horse has been tamed it can perform its tasks without harming anyone. However, if the horse remains untamed it may cause harm and be of no use to its owner.

Directed competition leads to an organized market. The illusion of the "free" market is propagated so that the few can benefit from this so-called freedom by enjoying the fruits of the labour of others (Chomsky, 2016a, 2016b).

On the other hand, a state regulated market is a historical anachronism and is viewed as contributing, amongst other things, to the fall of the Soviet Union and the collapse of Eastern Europe. However, directed competition and the organized market can use energy to "tame the wild horse".

For several thousand years, the market has been the starting point for trade and value creation. The organized market balances the various trends in the market, maintains competition and promotes value creation for the benefit of an increasing number of people (Pilger, 2016; De Sario, 2007).

Unless global market forces are tamed, the social consequences of free market thinking and hyper-competition may lead to self-destruction of the system as mentioned above in the reference to Zappfe's paradox, i.e. it's what you are good at that will be your downfall. Hyper-competition needs to be directed and the market organized, precisely so as to promote freedom, competition and market thinking. If balancing mechanisms are not installed to control some of the competition processes, then competition will cease to work (Dorling, 2015; Gant, 2014).

Global hyper-competition without global balancing social mechanisms may in its consequences lead to a sneaking introduction of various types of mandarin governance, and the development of a new type of capitalism, i.e. feudal capitalism. This will probably lead to an economic El-Nino literally causing the destruction of people's livelihoods and homes around the globe (Chomsky, 2016b; Ikonen, 2015). To use another analogy, giving free rein to financial capital may be likened to letting a fox into the henhouse.

Unique competence

One of the most important driving forces in the fourth industrial revolution is technological cutting edge expertise (Roat, 2016). It will therefore be extremely important for individuals, groups, organizations and nations to develop specific areas of expertise in which they possess unique competence. In the global economy, mediocrity, regardless of the level of education, will not constitute a competitive advantage. The skills that are developed must continually match what is demanded globally, because global demands will always materialise locally: i.e. the glocal (global + local) economic impact of the fourth industrial revolution.

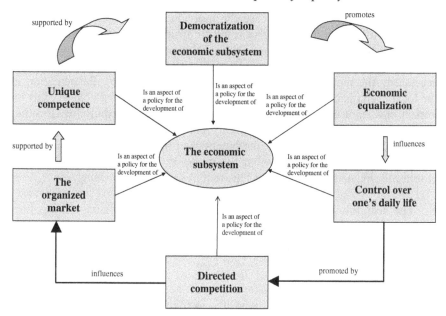

Figure 4.2 Aspects of a policy for the economic subsystem in the fourth industrial revolution

Summary

The economic subsystem's policy in the fourth industrial revolution is oriented around six elements described above and systematized in Figure 4.2.

The political subsystem

In this section, we investigate the question: Which policy can be developed for the political subsystem so that the fourth industrial revolution will lead to greater value creation for the benefit of an increasing number of people?

In the following, three elements will be discussed as aspects of a policy for the political subsystem of the fourth industrial revolution. The three elements are: power to the front-line, freedom from violation and activation requirements.

Power to the front-line and freedom from violation

It is incorrect to argue that it is the democratic system that is under pressure in the global knowledge economy (Johnson, 2015; Kessler, 2017). It is rather people's lack of influence over the processes that affect their everyday lives leading to their passivity and lack of engagement (Lazzarato, 2012; Mason, 2012, 2015). Such an understanding leads to completely different action strategies and policy design than the assumption that democracy is under any kind of pressure.

New developments that increase the individual's participation in the processes that affect him/her will also result in an increase in their participation
in democratic processes (Tarrow, 2005; Tolonen, 2005). It is being able to
influence the processes affecting one's daily life that are of interest here, not
necessarily the fact that the processes are local (Trot, 2015). Participation in
the local arena is not necessarily more democratic than being able to exert an
impact in distant decision-making forums that affect one's daily life. In other
words, democracy does not necessarily concern something that is locally
located but rather is to do with the potential of influencing the processes that
affect one's life, regardless of what the processes may be or if they are geo-
graphically located at a distance. This requires at least two things:

1   The technological opportunity to participate in decision-making pro-
    cesses that affect one's daily life.
2   Trust in the fact that people know what is best for them, and then acting
    in accordance with what they believe.

Thus, it is not a question of near or distant geographic location but greater
opportunity to influence one's daily life, no matter where the processes have
their geographical location (Varga, 2015; Savage, 2015). If one manages to
develop such democratic processes, then there is the possibility that this will
reduce the instances where people feel violated (Bennis et al., 2012).

One consequence of globalization is "tribalism", i.e. emotional commitment
to that which is local, ethnic identity, patriotism, nationalism, the individual's
own roots, myths, local narratives and knowledge of one's own history,
understanding of one's language and culture, and the personal (Reich, 2015;
Wiedemer et al., 2015). It is in this context that freedom from perceived violation
must be given priority before the said violation takes undesired directions
(Avent, 2016; Johnson, 2015).

Tribalism is based on solidarity between certain groups of people, where
the loyalty is to the group and not to the nation or global structures (Rozenblit, 2008). Democratic developments in various countries may be influenced
by the activities of these groups. Examples of this are the French-speaking
community in Canada; the Northern Ireland Conflict; the Basques in Spain;
the Kurds in Turkey, Iran and Iraq; the Spanish-speaking community in the
US; the Christians in Southern Sudan, etc. The identity that tribalism promotes
can shatter existing structures at the national level and affect the development
of collaborative structures at the global level (James, 2006). New technology,
including robotization, digitalization, informatization and automation, may
reinforce the focus on the local, the group and tribalism, i.e. on "us against
them" (de Anca, 2012). This may be explained as viewed from two perspectives:
firstly, because cultures are being globalized, thus promoting local involvement (Nordberg, 2016), and secondly, because the new technology enables
strong structural connections (Brynjolfsson & McAfee, 2014). These structural links can constitute a social mechanism for the rapid mobilization of

local involvement. There are at least two types of mobilizations: that which rises to the surface and is visible, and that which does not show itself but remains more hidden. The hidden mobilization enables the maintenance of the feeling of "belonging to the tribe", because contacts can be maintained in new ways. The new technology enables structural links and identity across geographic distances because identity and background are similar (Nordberg, 2016). With such a backdrop, it is reasonable to assume that respect for the individual and the safeguarding of the dignity of the individual, as well as responsibility for others, will be strengthened. Such a development will, in all likelihood, strengthen people's perceived dignity, reduce perceived violations and mitigate undesired actions (Benhabib, 2002, 2004; Benhabib et al., 2006).

The activation requirement

It is not a desirable solution to pay people to be passive, thus excluding them from social responsibility, simply because they for some reason are unable to fulfil what is a negotiated norm, such as an 8-hour work day (Bolanski & Chiapello, 2017).

The more active people are in relation to the processes that influence their own daily lives, the greater the likelihood of real power over their own lives (Beck, 2015). Activating those who are affected by the consequences of political processes will become a principal political task in the global knowledge economy (Sennett, 2003, 2013). However, activation will not necessarily be realized as a consequence of increased decentralization (Beck, 2015). In this context, the question is whether decentralization is of any real significance or whether there are other processes that have a greater impact on people's lives. It is the activation of those who are affected, which is of interest in the democratization of decision-making processes in the fourth industrial revolution (Bennis, et al., 2012). If activation is not increased and people do not gain more influence over their own lives, centralization of power may fall into the hands of a small minority (Bauman, 2013; Beck, 2015). This will only increase the distance between people and those that govern them, between the political and economic elite and those who do not belong to the elite (McGill, 2016). It seems reasonable to assume that increasing democratization in the fourth industrial revolution will place greater demands on the individual's activation in exchange for social benefits (Sennett, 2003; Savage, 2015). Thus, in the near future it seems probably that the individual citizen will be required to participate actively in return for their social benefits (Beck, 2015; Sennett, 2013). This could reduce the gap between those who govern and those who are governed, and it will also contribute to lessening the conflict between the elite and the others.

Summary

The political subsystem's policy in the fourth industrial revolution is oriented around the elements described above and systematized in Figure 4.3.

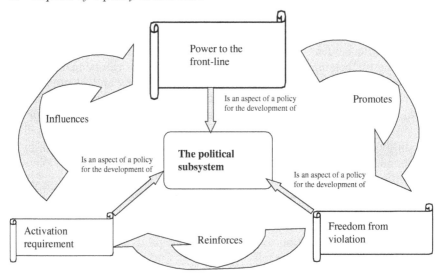

Figure 4.3 Aspects of a policy for the political subsystem in the fourth industrial revolution

The cultural subsystem

In this section we investigate the question: Which policy can be developed for the cultural subsystem so that the fourth industrial revolution will lead to greater value creation for the benefit of an increasing number of people?

In the following, three elements are discussed which are intended as aspects of a policy for the cultural subsystem in the fourth industrial revolution. The three elements are: respect for the individual, the dignity of the individual and responsibility for others.

Respect for the individual

In the beginning of the fourth industrial revolution, there is much to suggest that greater focus will be placed on respect for the individual (Benhabib, 2002, 2004; Benhabib et al., 2006).

In the industrial society, we often placed people in a waiting position. Figuratively this may be imagined to be in a warehouse where they were stored away like some machine part until they were needed; sometimes they would be taken out of storage, at other times people would be kept in storage their whole lives. If respect for the individual is to be a fundamental principle of the fourth industrial revolution, where competence is the most important social value creation mechanism, the above type of thinking that characterized the industrial society is both unethical (Benhabib, 2004) and of little use (Beck, 2015).

In the industrial society it was possible, perhaps even desirable, and in any case a common practice, to abandon what was considered to be "worn out" – parts that could be replaced with newer parts (Ackoff, 1989). Similarly, as mentioned, people were also treated like interchangeable machine parts (Bauman, 2011). However, if this way of thinking is adopted in the knowledge society, it may be likened to closing down half a library so that the books will not be worn out from being used. In this context, it is one's thinking that is problematic and not the actual phenomenon (Armano & Murgia, 2015: 102–117; Boxall & Purcell, 2010). The phenomenon in this case is people's competence. If this is to be transformed into value creation for the individual and society, it is a question of what is the most effective organization (Kessler, 2017).

When people are treated with respect and dignity, this forms the basis for social activation, involvement, participation and commitment (Benhabib, 2002, 2004; Sennett, 2013). Being active in cultural, political and economic value creation processes is a question of degree. This will depend on the individual's capabilities and background. It is this aspect that is of interest in the organization of the knowledge society (McAfee & Brynjolfsson, 2017). No one needs to be "stored away" for shorter or longer periods. It is rather a question of what is the most effective organization that can take full advantage of an individual's competence, although this competence may not fulfil certain "norms" such as the 8-hour work-day (Sennett, 2013).

In the industrial society, employees were active on the basis of a specific productivity norm. In the knowledge society, however, people can be active on the basis of a competence norm. Organized in this way, everybody will have the opportunity of being active on the basis of their background and capabilities, but never inactive. This will also result in the individual being treated with respect (Benhabib, 2004).

New developments suggest that identity appears to be veering away from the collective (Varga, 2015; Trot, 2015). The focus now seems to be on developing the skills needed for a particular job or task, but also the need of skills and knowledge to work with the new technology (Davenport & Kirby, 2005). In such a situation, it seems reasonable to assume that the social contract based on responsibility for the collective will become less prominent (Meister & Mulcahy, 2017: 1–15). More attention will be focused on the individual, and respect for the individual will be strengthened in such a context (Bauman, 2011). On the other hand, responsibility for, participation in and commitment to the collective will be given less emphasis (Castells, 2015). Although the focus will be more on the individual, it is not necessarily the case that the dignity of the individual will receive more attention (Charnock & Starosta, 2016).

If respect for the individual is to be given more emphasis, an action strategy may be to give the individual greater opportunity to choose his/her own future, although this may lead to collective solutions being put under pressure (Sennett, 2013; Beck, 2015).

The dignity of the individual

When unemployment becomes an integral part of the organization of society, responsibility for others is disregarded, and the dignity of the individual is violated (Chomsky, 2016a, 2016b).

It seems reasonable to assume that the perspective on unemployment is shifting in the knowledge society because competence has become the main input factor and the most important output factor (Morris, 2012; Nordberg, 2016). The same should also apply to the perspective on senior workers because their experience-based skills can be of importance as part of skills development in the institutions that develop skills, and in the systems that use this competence. Therefore, several ways of organizing experience transfer and knowledge building may be used where senior workers become part of this process. In this way, rather than being shuffled into retirement, senior workers will be able to actively participate in working life, albeit on different conditions than before. It is not only more rational to use the expertise of people that is available, no matter at which stage the person is in their life cycle, it will also show respect and strengthen his or her dignity by including them in key social activities (Sennett, 2013).

It lessens human dignity when people are hidden away in unemployment queues, receiving benefits on various social security schemes of imagined usefulness, and when healthy people are shuffled into retirement. Age is not a sickness, so those who are able and willing to work should be given the opportunity to participate in value creation activities in one way or another.

Responsibility for others

Flexibility is a significant dimension in the knowledge society (Pearson, 2015; Perlin, 2011). The reason is that competence is the key to value creation processes. Competence development is under continuous change in the fourth industrial revolution, and may therefore appear threatening to the individual (Rojecki, 2016; Avent, 2016). Therefore, individuals, organizations and society need to organize regarding values and standards in such a way that flexibility is a key factor for activities (Lele, 2011).

This flexibility can, amongst other things, be expressed in the way work is organized (Reinmoell & Reinmoeller, 2015). This could apply to people who suffer from a disability, who have reduced working capacity, and also in relation to senior workers (60+). It may be imagined that changing roles in working life could include senior workers, such as where they take on roles involving the coaching and supervising of younger workers. A mentor role would naturally replace a more active role for senior workers in the knowledge society.

Historically, unemployment has been a recurring phenomenon throughout the industrial era. This need not be the case in the knowledge society. Important in this context is flexibility during the course of one's working lifecycle regarding the development of knowledge, the application of knowledge and, towards the end of one's working lifecycle, the transfer of knowledge and experience.

People are not considered to be unemployed when at some point in their lives they are acquiring knowledge, such as in school or university – similarly, in the case mentioned above where senior workers (65+) transfer their knowledge and experience in roles as mentors or coaches, or perform other tasks. In the knowledge society, it is precisely competence that will be subject to continuous renewal because turbulence and complexity will increase. Such thinking is also linked to taking responsibility for others, as well as showing respect to seniors so that they can live worthwhile lives.

Summary

The cultural subsystem's policy in the fourth industrial revolution is oriented around the elements described above and systematized in Figure 4.4.

The social subsystem

In this section we investigate the question: Which policy can be developed for the collaborative system so that the fourth industrial revolution will lead to greater value creation for the benefit of an increasing number of people?

We discuss five elements in the following. These are: global competence clusters; collaborative networks; social inclusion; social justice; and social participation.

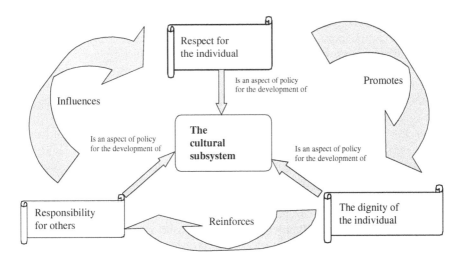

Figure 4.4 Aspects of a policy for the cultural subsystem in the fourth industrial revolution

Global competence clusters and collaborative networks

Firstly, a new aspect of global competence clusters is that they are distributed differently than previous international networks of various types (Abrahamson, 2004). Secondly, they are more structurally linked so that changes in one place more easily impact on other places in the network and/or in other global competence clusters (Avent, 2016). It is the new technology that facilitates and largely drives the global competence clusters (Wilson, 2017; Zhao et al., 2017). The global competence clusters may be likened to fishing nets lying on top of each other in a stack. Each fishing net constitutes a global competence cluster. The fishing nets are also in contact with each other along the vertical plane. This figurative image aims to elucidate how the separate global competence clusters are also structurally linked to other global competence clusters. In this way, it is possible to talk about the degree of internal structural links in the individual global competence clusters, and the degree of external structural links between the individual global competence clusters. The latter is illustrated by the connections between the fishing nets in the image described above.

Indeed, the better the external structural links are in the global competence clusters, the greater the level of expertise the network will have (Wilson, 2017). Global competence clusters will change the way we think, how we think, what we think, who we work with and the actions that result from this thinking and collaboration (Wakeling & Savage, 2015a, 2015b). The global competence clusters will form an organizational innovation in the global space, which will have an impact on value creation in the fourth industrial revolution (Susskind & Susskind, 2015).

Four types of collaborative networks may be envisaged (Bunge, 1998): the economic, political, social and cultural. The cultural collaborative networks will largely be based on personal relationships involving strong and weak ties. Similarly, the economic collaborative networks will also be dependent on personal relationships to strengthen performance because trust will replace controlling mechanisms (Castells, 2009). Thus, the global competence networks may be envisaged as strengthening personal relationships, both locally and globally. At the same time, globalization will erode existing bonds and change others. Geographical location will no longer be the basis for the fostering of personal relationships. The new collaborative networks will develop new links between people and new cultural expressions (Castells, 2015). Personal networks based on the relationships between good neighbours will in all probability be partly replaced by personal networks across geographical distances (Charnock & Starosta, 2016). In other words, social systems will develop that are no longer dependent on geographical location but will be based on various types of collaborative relationships in virtual space (Dickinson, 2016).

Figuratively, the development described above may be imagined as a chronological historical fast motion film showing the earth's globe. In the present and past, where the national borders exist, relationships and collaboration are etched in as dynamic dimensions changing gradually over time.

In the present and future, the fast motion film will show how national boundaries are softened with the passage of time and gradually replaced by networks of various types across borders. In terms of social consequences, new social systems will evolve over time based on these global clusters of competence. These may be envisioned as spreading out like waterfalls on this fast motion film across the aforesaid borders. If the development of various information and communication flows are also then etched onto this globe, a new reality would appear where the national borders are only of historical interest (Sennett, 2003).

Social relations have acquired a new character based on the new collaborative networks (Sennett, 2013). Therefore, new social systems will have other social matrices than those of the national state. How identity and loyalty are shaped may also then take on a different character (Castells, 2015).

Social inclusion, social justice and social participation

Solidarity in the knowledge society may be transformed into a more rational solidarity, i.e., solidarity will be viewed as something that directly benefits the individual (Sennett, 2013, Florida, 2014). This type of solidarity concurs with the increased individualization which we can observe at the start of the fourth industrial revolution (Goodman, 2015). However, individualization must not be confused with egoism. It seems reasonable to assume that individual solutions may also result in improved social justice. In the industrial society, the core of solidarity was also self-interest. The difference is that while rational solidarity is based on individual solutions, traditional solidarity takes as its starting point collective solutions. It is not, therefore, a weakening of solidarity that will emerge in the knowledge society – it will only become more explicit who it benefits (Bauman, 2011, 2013).

Clear solutions to complex issues appear to be the preferred approach, rather than complex solutions. This is because clear solutions will provide greater transparency, which will also facilitate social participation (Sennett, 2013; Castells, 2015). On the other hand, clear solutions should not be confused with simple and easy ones. Improved communication and system integration may be used to reduce complexity, reduce uncertainty about information, and minimize ambiguity (Luhmann, 1996; Bunge, 2015). Complexity may also be reduced by integrating all the systems operating within the specific problem area, such as the school, the family, the police and healthcare.

Intervention will involve systemic integration, i.e. responsibility for the part and whole of the person it concerns (Bunge, 1998). This may be done through integrating the entire life of the person in focus. It is precisely integration that is desirable to achieve the necessary intervention. The integration of the insular professional institutions and the structural links between the various professions will provide the opportunity to increase the quality of life of the individual. In this way, social participation will be encouraged because solution strategies will become transparent, connected and clear.

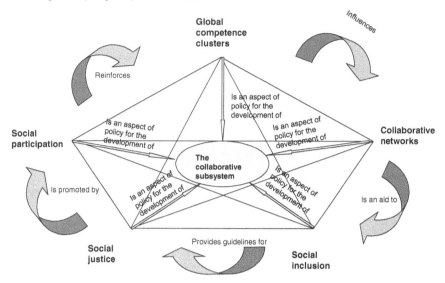

Figure 4.5 Aspects of a policy for the collaborative system in the fourth industrial revolution

Summary

Aspects of a policy for the collaborative system in the fourth industrial revolution will be oriented around the elements described above and systematized in Figure 4.5.

Conclusion

The research question we have investigated in this chapter is the following: Which overall policy can be developed so that the fourth industrial revolution will lead to greater value creation for the benefit of an increasing number of people?

In brief, we have designed 17 policy interventions, which comprises: six for the economic subsystem, three for the political subsystem, three for the cultural subsystem and five for the collaborative system. Based on the investigation in this chapter, we have illustrated the response to the research question in Table 4.1.

Theoretical and practical implications

Changes in bureaucratic management and control structures are considered to be a major challenge at the start of the fourth industrial revolution. Traditional management ideology is associated with the industrial society, and is

Table 4.1 Policy interventions in the fourth industrial revolution

Social subsystem	Expressed through	Aspects of a policy for the fourth industrial revolution
The economic subsystem	Material resources	Democratization of the economic subsystem Economic equalization Control over one's daily life Directing competition The organized market Unique competence
The political subsystem	Power	Power to the front-line Freedom from violation Activation requirement
The cultural subsystem	Values	Respect for the individualThe dignity of the individual Responsibility for others
The collaborative subsystem	Human relations	Global competence network Collaborative networks Social inclusion Social justice Social participation

neither possible nor desirable in the globalized knowledge economy. It is not possible because information and knowledge processes are largely driven by the front-line of the system. It is not desirable because it will suffocate initiative and creativity. However, this does not mean that management and control are not possible or desirable. It is possible precisely because self-organization enables management by those who have the expertise and operate in the front-line. It is desirable because the possible outcomes are infinite and complexity needs to be reduced.

It seems reasonable to assume that the economic aspect of globalization will lead to increased tensions, due to differences between profits and wages. This may occur in both the countries where the new industrialization is growing, and in the old industrialized countries that are being transformed into knowledge economies. The knowledge economies will increasingly base their value creation on robots, informats and artificial intelligence.

In the same way that we learned to live with uncertainty in the industrial society, we must learn to live with ambiguity in the knowledge society. Uncertainty was dealt with through using information. Ambiguity may be reduced by communication. Multicultural involvement will be an aid for learning how to deal with ambiguity, because the knowledge society operates in the global space, which by definition is multicultural. In such a global world, cultural identity becomes important. However, cultural identity must not be confused with cultural protectionism (Chomsky, 2016a, 2016b). Cultural protectionism can take many isolating and excluding forms. Cultural protectionism may easily descend into national protectionism that excludes those who do not "belong" in the national space. The worst forms of cultural protectionism belong to the darkest sides of European history.

Identity grows literally over time as a distinction between a system and its external world. It is important to be aware of which cultural identity one wishes to create and to show to others. Cultural identity is what distinguishes us from others. However, one should be aware that there is a delicate balance between distinguishing oneself from others and separating oneself from them. The latter is the expression of cultural protectionism.

Creolization, also known as cultural pluralism, is a balancing mechanism that can ensure that cultural identity does not descend into cultural protectionism. Creolization is the multicultural expression of respect, responsibility and dignity. Creolization offers protection against intolerance, oppression, violation and exclusionary attitudes.

In the knowledge society, competence is possibly the most important input factor for value creation. In order to attract competent people, you need a culture that is appealing. Consequently, culture may become the most important factor when attracting competence because it relates to the identity of others. In order to compete in the global market, it is crucial that social systems have the best skills within their defined area. Taking this into consideration, culture is not so much the result of the economic development of a country, but something that needs to be fostered so it appears as appealing and provides a basis for value creation.

Notes

1 Informats are robots which are globally interconnected. In this way they continuously acquire new information within the functional area.
2 The philosopher Zappfe formulated (in brief) the following paradox: It's what you are good at that will be your downfall
3 https://en.wikipedia.org/wiki/Input–output_model (access date: 28.3.2017). Leontief was awarded the Nobel Prize in Economics in 1973.

References

Abd, K.K. (2017). *Intelligent scheduling of robotic flexible assembly cells*, Springer, London.

Abrahamson, M. (2004). *Global cities*, Oxford University Press, Oxford.

Ackoff, R.L. (1989). *Re-creating the corporate future*, Oxford University Press, Oxford.

Antonelli, V. (2001). *The microeconomics of technological change*, Oxford University Press, Oxford.

Armano, E. & Murgia, A. (2015). The precariousness of young knowledge workers: a subject-oriented approach, in Johnson, M. (Ed.). *Precariat: labour, work and politics*, Routledge, London, pp. 102–117.

Avent, R. (2016). *The wealth of humans: work and its absence in the twenty-first century*, Allen Lane, New York.

Banki, S. (2015). Precarity of place: a complement to the growing precariat literature, in Johnson, M. (Ed.). *Precariat: labour, work and politics*, Routledge, London, pp. 66–79.

Bauman, Z. (2011). *Culture in a liquid modern world*, Polity Press, London.

Bauman, Z. (2013). *Does the richness of the few benefit us all?* Polity, London.

Beck, U. (1992). *Risk society: towards a new modernity*, Sage, London.

Beck, U. (2015). *Reinvention of politics: rethinking modernity in the global social order*, Polity, New York.

Beer, S. (1979). *The heart of enterprise*, John Wiley & Sons, Chichester.

Beer, S. (1981). *Brain of the firm*, John Wiley & Sons, New York.

Beer, S. (1995). *Diagnosing the system for organizations*, John Wiley & Sons, London.

Benhabib, S. (2002). *The claims of culture*, Princeton University Press, Princeton.

Benhabib, S. (2004). *The rights of others*, Cambridge University Press, Cambridge.

Benhabib, S., Waldron, J., Honig, B. & Kymlicka, W. (eds.) (2006). *Another cosmopolitanism*, Oxford University Press, Oxford.

Bennis, W.G., Cloke, K. & Goldsmith, J. (2012). *The end of management and the rise of organizational democracy*, John Wiley & Sons, New York.

Biswas-Diener, R. (2011). *Positive psychology and social change*, Springer, London.

Bolanski, L. & Chiapello, E. (2017). *The new spirit of capitalism*, Verso, London.

Boxall, P.F. & Purcell, J. (2010). An HRM perspective on employee participation, in Wilkinson, A., Golan, P.J., Marchington, M. & Lewins, D. (eds.). *The Oxford handbook of participation in organizations*, Oxford University Press, Oxford, pp. 129–151.

Brynjolfsson, E. & McAfee, A. (2014). *The second machine age*, W.W. Norton & Company, New York.

Bunge, M. (1998). *Philosophy of science: from problem to theory*, Volume one, Transaction Publishers, New Jersey.

Bunge, M. (2015). *Political philosophy*, Transaction Publisher, New York.

Case, S. (2016). *The third wave*, Simon & Schuster, New York.

Castelfranchi, C. (2007). Six critical remarks on science and the construction of the knowledge society, *Journal of Science Communication*, 6(4), 1–3.

Castells, M. (2009). *The power of identity*, Wiley-Blackwell, Oxford.

Castells, M. (2015). *Networks of outrage and hope*, Polity Press, New York.

Charnock, G. & Starosta, G. (2016). *The new international division of labour, global transformation and uneven development*, Palgrave, London.

Chomsky, N. (2012). *How the world works*, Hamish Hamilton, London.

Chomsky, N. (2016a). *Profit over people: war against people*, Piper, Berlin.

Chomsky, N. (2016b). *Who rules the world*, Hamish Hamilton, London.

Davenport, T. H. & Kirby, J. (2005). *Only humans need apply: winners & losers in the age of smart machines*, Harper Business, New York.

Davies, A.C. (2003). Are firms moving Downstream into High-Value Services? In Tidd, J. & Hull, F.M. *Service innovation: organizational responses to technological opportunities & market imperatives.* Imperial College Press, London, pp 321–340.

De Anca, C. (2012). *Beyond tribalism*, Palgrave, London.

De Sario, B. (2007). Precari Su Marte: an experiment in activism against precarity, *Feminist Review*, 87, 1: 21–39.

Florida, R. (2014). *The rise of the creative class*, Basic Books, New York.

Dickinson, E. (2016). *Globalization and migration*, Rowman & Littlefield, London.

Dorling, D. (2015). *Inequality and the 1%*, Verso, London.

Drucker, P.F. (1999a). Knowledge worker productivity: the biggest challenge, *California Management Review*, 41, 2: 79–94.

Drucker, P.F. (1999b). *Management challenges for the 21st century*. Harper Collins, New York.

Gans, J. (2016). *The disruption dilemma*, The MIT Press, Boston.

Gant, A. (2014). *Give and take, Why helping others drives our success*, W&N, New York.

Gollan, P.J. (2010). Employer strategies towards non-union collective voice, in Wilkinson, A., Golan, P.J., Marchington, M. & Lewins, D. (eds.). *The Oxford handbook of participation in organizations*, Oxford University Press, Oxford, pp. 212–236.

Goodman, J. (2015). *Crisis, movement, management: globalising dynamics*, Routledge, London.

Gupta, S., Habjan, J. & Tutek, H. (2016). *Academic labour unemployment and global higher education: neoliberal politics of funding and management*, Palgrave, London.

Harrison, G. & Freeman, R. (2004). Democracy in and around organizations, *The Academy of Management Journal*, 18, 3: 49–53.

Harvey, D. (2007). *A brief history of neoliberalism*, Oxford University Press, Oxford.

Hills, J., Sefton, T. & Stewart, K. (2009). *Towards a more equal society*, Policy Press, Bristol.

Ikonen, K-M. (2015). Precarious work, entrepreneurial mindset and the sense of place: female strategies in insecure labour markets, in Johnson, M. (Ed.). *Precariat: labour, work and politics*, Routledge, London, pp. 83–97.

James, P. (ed.). (2006) *Globalism, nationalism, tribalism: bringing theory back in*, Sage, New York.

Johnson, M. (2015). Introduction, the precariat, in Johnson, M. (Ed.). *Precariat: labour, work and politics*, Routledge, London, pp. 1–3.

Kessler, S. (2017). *Gigged: the end of jobs and the future of work*, Random House Business, New York.

Lazzarato, M. (2012). *The making of indebted man: an essay of the neoliberal condition*, Semiotext E, San Francisco.

Lele, C.G. (2011). *Organizational democracy: collaborative team culture: key to organizational growth*, Atlantic Publisher, New York.

Luhmann, N. (1996). *Social systems*, Stanford University Press, Stanford.

Mason, P. (2012). *Why it's kicking off everywhere: the new global revolutions*, Verso, New York.

Mason, P. (2015). *Postcapitalism: a guide to our future*, Allen Lane, London.

McAfee, A. & Brynjolfsson, E. (2017). *Machine platform: harnessing the digital revolution*, W.W. Norton Company, New York.

McGill, K. (2016). *Global inequality*, University of Toronto Press, Toronto.

Meister, J.C. & Mulcahy, K.J. (2017). *The future workplace experience*, McGraw Hill, New York.

Morris, J. (2012). Unruly entrepreneurs: Russian worker responses to insecure formal employment, *Global Labour Journal*, 3, 2: 217–236.

Nordberg, K. (2016). *Revolutionizing economic and democratic systems: reinventing the third way*, Palgrave, New York.

Pearson, T. (2015). *The end of jobs*, Lioncrest Publishing, New York.

Perlin, R. (2011). *Intern nation: how to earn nothing and learn little in the brave new economy*, Verso, London.

Petras, J. & Veltmeyr, H. (2011). *Beyond neoliberalism: a word to win*, Routledge, London.

Petras, J., Veltmeyr, H. & Marquez, H. (2013). *Imperialism and capitalism in the twenty-first century: a system of crises*, Routledge, London.

Piketty, T. (2014). *Capital in the twenty-first century*, Belknap, Boston.

Piketty, T. (2016). *Chronicles: on our troubled times*, Viking, London.

Pilger, J. (2016). *The new rulers of the world*, Verso, London.

Reich, R. (2015). *Saving capitalism*, Alfred. A. Knopf, New York.

Reinmoell, S. & Reinmoeller, P. (2015). *The ambidextrous organization*, Routledge, Oxford.

Roat, H. (2016). *Capital and collusion: the political logic of global economic development*, Princeton University Press, Princeton.

Rodrik, D. (2011). *The globalization paradox*, Oxford University Press, Oxford.

Rojecki, A. (2016). *America and the politics of insecurity*, John Hopkins University Press, New York.

Rosa, H. & Mathys-Treio, J. (2015). *Social acceleration*, Columbia University Press, New York.

Rozenblit, B. (2008). *Us against them. How tribalism affects the way we think*, Transcendent Publication, New York.

Savage, M. (2015). *Social class in the 21st century*, Penguin, London.

Schwab, K. (2016). *The fourth industrial revolution*, World Economic Forum, Geneva.

Sennett, R. (2003). *The fall of public man*, Penguin, New York.

Sennett, R. (2013). *Together*, Penguin, New York.

Susskind, R. & Susskind, D. (2015). *The future of professions: how technology will transform the work of human experts*, Oxford University Press, Oxford.

Tarrow, S. (2005). *The new transnational activism*, Cambridge University Press, Cambridge.

Tolonen, T. (2005). Locality and gendered capital of working-class youth, *Young*, 13, 4: 343–361.

Trot, B. (2015). From the precariat to the multitude, in Johnson, M. (Ed.). *Precariat: labour, work and politics*, Routledge, London, pp. 22–41.

Varga, J.J. (2015). Breaking the heartland. Creating the precariat in the US lower rust belt, in Johnson, M. (Ed.). *Precariat: labour, work and politics*, Routledge, London, pp. 46–62.

Wakeling, P. & Savage, M. (2015a). Elite universities, elite schooling and reputation in Britain, in Zanten, A.V. & Ball, S. *Elites, privilege and excellence: the national and global redefinition of educational advantage, world yearbook of education*, Abingdon, London.

Wakeling, P. & Savage, M. (2015b). Entry to elite positions and the stratification of higher education in Britain, *Sociological Review*, 63, 2: 290–320.

Wiedemer, D., Wiedemer, R.A. & Spitzer, C. S. (2015). *Aftershock*, Wiley, London.

Wilson, M. (2017). *Implementation of robot systems*, Butterworth-Heinemann, New York.

Zhao, J., Feng, Z., Chu, F. & Ma, N. (2017). *Advanced theory of constraint and motion analysis for robot mechanisms*, Academic Press, London.

5   Concepts

Ambidextrous organizations

Ambidextrous organizations are organizations that have the ability to adapt to changes in external conditions while at the same time generating their own future by means of, among other things, performance improvement, growth and innovation (Duncan, 1976; O'Reilly & Tushman, 2004; 2007; 2011; Thota & Munir, 2011). In Chapter X, we have shown how ambidextrous organizations can be developed by HR departments.

In 2004, O'Reilly & Tushman expressed that ambidextrous organizations would constitute one of the major challenges for management in the global knowledge economy.

The findings of O'Reilly & Tushman (2004) were overwhelming. Regarding the launching of radical innovations, they found that none of the cross-functional or unsupported teams and only a quarter of the teams with functional designs were able to produce radical innovations. However, among the ambidextrous organizations, 90% were successful in producing radical innovations. Empirical research has shown that this type of organizational design is best for producing both incremental and radical innovations.

Asplund's motivation theory[1]

In brief, this theory can be described in the following way: *People are motivated by social responses* (Asplund, 2010: 221–229). The following statement may be said to be a central point made by Asplund's theory: *When people receive social responses, their level of activity increases.*

Asplund's motivation theory is consistent with North's action theory (rcf. North's action theory). Understood in this way, it seems reasonable to connect the two theories in the statement: *People are motivated by the social responses rewarded by the institutional framework.*

Availability cascades

This refers to the idea that we are all controlled by the image of reality created by the media, because this image is easy to retrieve from memory.

Availability proposition

This may be expressed as follow: the more easily information enters into our consciousness, the greater the likelihood that we will have confidence in that information. In other words, we believe more in the type of information that is available in memory than the information that is not so readily available.

Behavioural perspective

This perspective focuses on the behaviour of employees as an explanation for the relationship between business strategy and the results obtained.

Boudon-Coleman diagram

This research methodology was developed by Mario Bunge (Bunge, 1977: 76–79) based on insights made by the sociologists Boudon and Coleman. The purpose of the diagram is to show the relationship between the various levels, such as the macro- and micro-levels. For instance, it is shown how changes at the macro-level, such as technological innovations in feudal society, can lead to increased income at the micro-level. However, it was shown that technological innovations could lead to weakening of the semi-feudal structures because dependency on landowners was reduced. Consequently, the landowners opposed such changes especially in the case of technological innovations, which Boudon has shown in his research (Boudon, 1981: 100). Coleman (Coleman, 1990: 7–12) started at the macro-level, went to the individual level to find explanations and finally ended up at the macro-level again.

An important purpose of Bunge's Boudon-Coleman diagram is to identify social mechanisms that maintain or change the phenomenon or problem under investigation (as mentioned above, in Boudon's analysis of semi-feudal society). Bunge's Boudon-Coleman diagram may be said to represent a "mixed strategy"; Bunge says the following:

> When studying systems of any kind a) reduce them to their components (at some level) and the interaction among these, as well as among them and environmental items, but acknowledge and explain emergence (see the chapter on concepts) whenever it occurs, and b) approach systems from all pertinent sides and on all relevant levels, integrating theories or even research fields whenever unidisciplinarity proves to be insufficient.(Bunge, 1998: 78)

The purpose of this research strategy is to arrive at a deeper and more complete explanation of a system's behaviour.

Capabilities

Capabilities are for an organization what abilities are for an individual.

An organizational capability may thus be defined as an organization's ability to perform a task, activity or process. Operational capabilities enable an organization to make money in the here and now (Winter, 2003: 991–995). Dynamic capabilities, as opposed to operational capabilities, are linked to processes of change. Change and innovation are at the centre of dynamic capabilities.

Simplified, one may say that organizational capabilities are something an organization does well compared to its competitors (Ulrich and Brockbank, 2005). These capabilities are intangible and therefore difficult for competitors to imitate (Wernerfelt, 1984).

Cohesive energy

In a social system cohesive energy is "the glue" that binds the system together. Cohesive energy is the social mechanisms that make the system durable. According to systemic thinking it is the relationships and actions that bind social systems together. The rationale is that relationships and the systems of relationships may be said to control human behaviour. Social systems are held together (in systemic thinking) by dynamic social relations (e.g. feelings, perceptions, norms) and social action (e.g. cooperation, solidarity, conflict and communication).

Co-creation

Co-creation involves working together to promote knowledge processes and innovation. If knowledge processes and innovation are essential for value creation in the knowledge society, co-creation is an important social mechanism for initiating, maintaining and strengthening these processes. The balance between competition and cooperation, embodied in the concept of co-creation, leads to constructive criticism and the necessary scope of knowledge that exists in the network so as to promote creativity and the innovative. Instead of a zero-sum situation, a positive-sum situation will be developed where everyone wins.

Collective blindness

Collective blindness may be said to be a form of collective arrogance, which results in irrational actions. Minor events slip under the radar, causing the system to not be fully aware of what is happening. Politicians' explanations why voters in a referendum vote contrary to what most of the power elite and the media advocated is an example of collective blindness.

Competence

Competence refers to knowledge, skills and attitudes.

Core competence

The concept was popular in the strategy literature of the 1990s. Core competence may be defined as: "a bundle of skills and technologies that enable a company to provide a particular benefit to customers" (Hamel & Prahalad, 1996: 219). More recently, core competence as a concept has been given less attention in the research on dynamic capabilities, and now there is more focus on the concept of *fitness*. The term *evolutionary fitness* is also used in the research literature in connection with technology, quality, cost development, market development, innovation and competitive positioning (Helfat et al., 2007: 7).

Discontinuous innovations

These are innovations that change the premises of technology, markets, our mindset and so on. We know that sooner or later discontinuous innovations will emerge in the future (Hewing, 2013).

Dynamic capabilities

Dynamic capabilities stem from the resource-based perspective and evolutionary thinking in strategy literature (Teece, 2013: 3–65, 82–113; Nelson and Winter, 1982). The dynamic perspective attempts to explain what promotes an organization's competitive position over time through innovation and growth (Teece, 2013: x).

The original thinking concerning dynamic capabilities may be related to Teece et al. (1997). These authors defined dynamic capabilities as *an organization's ability to create, develop and modify its internal and external expertise in order to address changes in the external world.*

Dynamic capabilities are now seen as all the organizational processes, not only internal and external expertise, that contribute to an organization's capacity to adapt to change while creating the organization's future.

Explicit knowledge

This is knowledge that can be digitized and communicated to others as information.

Evidence

This may be results, such as research results, that can be relied on. However, it is also important to be aware of the fact that other evidence may be available without having to refer to figures and quantities, such as evidence that emerges from observations and good judgement without the assessment being quantified. Evidence-based research is research results that are based on approved and accepted scientific research methods.

Emergent

An emergent occurs if something new turns up on one level that has not previously existed on the level below. With emergent we mean: Let S be a system with composition A, i.e. the various components in addition to the way they are composed. If P is a property of S, P is emergent with regard to A, if and only if no components in A possess P; otherwise P is to be regarded as a resulting property with regards to A (Bunge, 1977: 97).

Entrepreneurial spirit

The entrepreneurial spirit may be described as follows (Roddick, 2003: 106–107):

- The vision of something new and belief in this that is so strong that belief becomes reality.
- A touch of positive madness.
- The ability to stand out from the crowd.
- Creative tension bubbling over.
- Pathological optimism.
- To act before you know!
- Basic desire for change.
- Creative energy focused on ideas, not on explicit factual knowledge.
- Being able to tell the story you want to sell.

Feedback

Giving the other person feedback, for instance with regard to their behaviour, attitudes and the like, is the most important element in the area of interactive skills and emotional intelligence (Goleman, 1996; 2007). Analysis of feedback is a sure way to identify our strengths and then reinforce them (Wang et al., 2003). Failure to give people feedback on their behaviour in some contexts may even be considered immoral.

Feed-forward

Feed-forward is regarded here as an expectation mechanism. It seems reasonable to assume that our expectations influence our behaviour in the present. It is therefore important that we make explicit to ourselves the expectations we have of a situation. By making expectations explicit, we have a greater opportunity to learn from our experiences and thus improve our performance.

Front-line focus

This refers to those in the front line, i.e. in direct contact with customers, users, patients, students, etc. They have the greatest expertise, necessary information and decision-making authority and are regarded as the most important resource in the organization because they are at the point where an organization's value creation occurs.

Global competence network

These competence networks may be divided into political, social, economic, technological and cultural patterns. It is when these five patterns interact that one may perceive the overall pattern. In the global knowledge economy it seems reasonable to assume that those who control this pattern set the conditions for economic development. These global competence networks will most likely make an impact on HR departments in companies competing for this kind of expertise in national markets.

Global competence networks are also emphasized as crucial for economic growth by OECD (2001), although they use the term *innovative clusters*. The purpose of innovative clusters and global competence networks is the development, dissemination and use of new ideas that promote wealth creation.

There is much to suggest that a greater degree of integration and cooperation between private and public sectors at the national and regional levels is an important prerequisite for initiating the innovative locomotive effect. The global competence networks are metaphorically the energy source that sustains the motion of this locomotive. It would be counterproductive to replace the locomotive once in motion. Conversely, the individual carriages of the locomotive (read: organizational level) can be changed depending on their competitive position. The individual passengers on the train create ideas and knowledge through the processes that may be called *creative chaos*. In this way we will arrive at a tripartite of the prerequisites for global competence networks. At the individual level, creative chaos occurs. At the organizational level, there will be creative destruction. At the social and global levels, creative collaboration takes place. These three processes create innovation and economic growth as an emergent, not as a *future perfectum*, i.e. a planned process with given results.

A prerequisite for the reasoning above is that tension and competition at one level requires collaboration at another level. Competition and cooperation are both necessary if one is to develop innovation and economic growth, in the same manner that stability and change are necessary for flexibility. Too much of the one (stability) leads to rigidity, and too much of the other (change) leads to chaos. Understood in this way, emergents cannot be planned.

Hamel's Law of Innovation

The "law" states that only between one and two of one thousand ideas become innovations in a market (Hamel, 2002; 2012). Therefore, an infostructure must be created to ensure that ideas are continuously produced in a business.

Hidden knowledge

Hidden knowledge is what we do not know we do not know. Kirzner (1982) says that hidden knowledge is possibly the most important knowledge domain of creativity, innovation and entrepreneurship.

History's "slow fields"

This refers to the fact that norms, values and actions tend to be in operation long after the functions, activities and processes that initially created them disappear, thus generating so-called *slow fields of history*. These norms, values and actions exist though they have no apparent function, contributing to maintaining a type of behaviour long after the type of behaviour is functional or meaningful.[2] For sociologists and historians it is important to determine whether norms and values have any function, or whether they are part of history's slow fields. By examining history's slow fields, it may be possible to provide better explanations for phenomena.

HR management

HR management is defined as HR practices at various levels (micro, meso, macro) for managing people in organizations.

HR management has been defined in many different ways. For instance, Boxall and Purcell (2003: 1) define HR management as all those activities oriented towards managing relations between employees in an organization. This definition emphasizes the relational perspective. Later, they expanded their definition to include all the activities and processes that underpin an organization's value creation (Boxall and Purcell, 2010: 29). On this basis, Armstrong defines the activities and processes that HR management should engage in:

> HRM covers activities such as human capital management, knowledge management, organizational design and development, resource planning (recruitment, talent development), performance management, organizational learning, reward systems, relationships between employees, and employees' wellness.(Armstrong, 2014: 6)

However, we believe Armstrong underestimates two essential areas of knowledge in his definition: the management of innovation processes, and change processes in organizations. Innovation and change are strongly emphasized in the global HRM survey (White & Younger, 2013: 35–39). Armstrong has included the ethical perspective in his handbook for HRM (Armstrong, 2014: 95–105). Management of innovation processes and change processes in organizations is also highlighted and underlined by Wright et al. (2011: 5) in their description of HRM. However, it must also be said that Armstrong discusses innovation (Armstrong, 2014: 145–155), but not in his process definition of HR management. Innovation and change processes are also emphasized by Ulrich et al. (2013a). Brockbank (2013: 24) especially mentions these two processes as being important in the research model Ulrich et al. (2013a) have developed through their empirical research over 25 years.

Implicit knowledge

This is knowledge that is spread throughout an organization but not integrated.

Informats

By informat, we mean robots with artificial intelligence which are inter-connected in a global technological network. Figuratively, informats may be imagined as clusters of neurons in the human brain, which are con-nected to other neuron-clusters to create the various functions of human intelligence (Wilson, 2017; Winfield, 2012; Vadakkepat & Goswami, 2018). In the financial world, the use of robots by financial analysts provides an example of the use of so-called informats. Informats for use in medical sur-gery are already on the drawing board and will be a reality in the near future (Bleuer et al., 2017); the same applies to the use of informats in the service and education sectors (Bleuer & Bouri, 2017). Informats are understood here in the context of the above description as being emergents[3] in relation to robots; informats can sense, analyse and reach decisions in the space of a micro-second.

Information input overload

This occurs when an individual, a team, an organization or a community receive more information than they can manage to process.

In a situation characterised by information input overload the following may occur (Miller, 1978: 123):

1 Designated tasks and responsibilities are left undone.
2 Errors are made.
3 Queues of information occur.
4 Information is filtered out that should have been included.
5 Abstract formulations are made when they should have been specific.
6 Communication channels are overloaded, creating stress and tension in the system.
7 Complex situations are shunned.
8 Information is lumped together for processing.

Each of the above eight points may result in a decrease in efficiency when the system is exposed to information input overload.

Informats

By informat, we mean robots with artificial intelligence which are interconnected in a global technological network. Figuratively, informats may be imagined as clusters of neurons in the human brain, which are connected to other neuron-clusters to create the various functions of human intelligence (Wilson, 2017; Winfield, 2012; Vadakkepat & Goswami, 2018). In the financial world, the use of robots by financial analysts provides an example of the use of so-called informats. Informats for use in medical surgery are already on the drawing board and will be a reality in the near future (Bleuer et al., 2017); the same applies to the use of informats in the service and education sectors (Bleuer & Bouri, 2017). Informats are understood here in the context of the above description as being emergents[4] in relation to robots; informats can sense, analyse and reach decisions in the space of a micro-second.

Infostructure

The infostructure concerns the processes that enable the development, transfer, analysis, storage, coordination and management of data, information and knowledge. The infostructure consists of eleven generic processes. The eleven processes in the infostructure may be considered as nodes in a social network at different levels, for example team, organization, society and region, all in the global space. Together, the eleven processes comprise the totality of the infostructure.

It may be said that the *info*structure has the same importance in the knowledge society as the *infra*structure had in the industrial society.

Innovation

Innovation is here understood as any idea, practice or material element, which is perceived as new for the person using it (Zaltman et al., 1973).

Ideas are seen as the smallest unit in the innovation process (Hamel, 2002; 2012). However, this refers to the ideas that are in process of development and not fully developed ideas. Before an idea can be characterized as innovative, it must prove to be beneficial to somebody, i.e. the market must accept the idea and apply it. Consequently, the creative process of innovation is here understood as the benefit it has for a market. Thus, it is not sufficient that an idea is new for it to be considered an innovation. An idea may have a great degree of novelty, but if it is of no benefit to anybody in the market, then it has no innovative value.

Kaizen

This is a Japanese method, which means that an organization develops systems for organized improvement.

Knowledge

The definition of knowledge used here is *the systematization and structuring of information for one or more goals or purposes.*

Knowledge enterprise

This is an enterprise that has knowledge as its most significant output. It is perhaps helpful to think of the process *input–process–output* to separate industrial enterprises from knowledge enterprises. Much knowledge and skills are needed to produce high-tech products such as computers, and there are also many knowledge workers involved in this process. However, the majority of products produced today are high-tech industrial products, and although such products require very skilled knowledge in the production process, they are nevertheless output-industrial products.

On the other hand, law firms, consulting firms and universities are examples of knowledge enterprises.

Knowledge management

Management of knowledge resources in an organization. These resources may be explicit knowledge, implicit knowledge, tacit knowledge and hidden knowledge.

Knowledge worker

A knowledge worker has been described by the OECD as *a person whose primary task is to generate and apply knowledge*, rather than to provide services or produce physical products (OECD, 2000a, 2000b, 2000c, 2000d, 2000e; 2001). This may be understood as a *formal definition* of a knowledge worker.

This definition does not restrict knowledge workers to creative fields, as is the case with, for example, Mosco and McKercher (2007: vii–xxiv). The OECD definition also allows for the fact that a knowledge worker may perform routine tasks. The definition also does not limit the type of work performed by knowledge workers to tasks relating to creative problem-solving strategies, unlike the definition provided by Reinhardt et al. (2011).

Locomotive effect

This refers to something that generates and then reinforces an activity or development.

Modularization

An extreme fragmentation of the production process in the global knowledge economy. Production is fragmented and distributed according to the following logic: costs–quality–competence–design–innovation.

Modular flexibility

The modulization of value creation. Modular flexibility may best be understood as the globalization of production processes, and extreme specialization of work processes with a focus on core processes.

Necessary and sufficient conditions

It may often be appropriate to divide conditions or premises into *necessary conditions* and *sufficient conditions*. Necessary conditions must be present to trigger an action, but these may not be sufficient. The sufficient conditions must also be present to trigger the action.

North's action theory[5]

This action theory may be expressed in the following statement: People act on the basis of a system of rewards as expressed in the norms, values, rules and attitudes in the culture (the institutional framework) (North, 1990; 1993). North's action theory is also consistent with Asplund's motivation theory (ref. Asplund's motivation theory).

Primary task

An organization's primary task is what the system is designed to do.

Proposition

This is an overarching hypothesis. It says something about the relationship between several variables. A proposition relates to a hypothesis in the same way the main research problem relates to research questions.

Punctuation

By punctuation (Bateson, 1972: 292–293) a distinction is drawn between cause and effect; this is done with a clear motive in mind. A causality is thus created which does not actually exist in the real world, and one is then free to discuss the effects of this cause which has been created through a process of punctuation.

A sequence of a process is selected, and then bracketed. In this way, we de-limit what is punctuated from the rest of the process. Figuratively, we may imagine this as a circle that is divided into small pieces; one piece of the circle is then selected and folded out into a straight line. This results in the creation of an artificial beginning and end. This beginning and end of course cannot exist in a circle, but only through the process of punctuation.

Social laws

Social laws constitute a pattern of a unique type. They are systemic and connected to a system of knowledge, and cannot change without the facts they represent also being changed (Bunge, 1983a; 1983b). The main differences between a statement of a law and other statements are:

1   Law statements are general.
2   Law statements are systemic, i.e. they are related to the established system of knowledge.
3   Law statements have been verified through many studies.

A pattern may be understood as variables that are stable over a specific period of time. A social law is created when an observer gains insight into the pattern. By gaining such insight, we can also predict parts of behaviour or at least develop a rough estimate within a short period of time.

Social laws are further related to specific social systems, both in time and space. However, this does not represent any objection to social laws, because this is also true of natural laws (although these have a longer time span and are of a more general nature).

Social mechanism

Robert Merton (1967) brought the notion of social mechanisms into sociology, although we can find rudiments of this in both Weber – with the Protestant ethic as an explanation for the emergence of capitalism in Europe – and in Durkheim, who uses society as an explanation for a rising suicide rate. For Merton, social mechanisms are the building blocks of *middle range theories*. He defines social mechanisms as *social processes having designated consequences for designated parts of the social structure* (Merton, 1967: 43). In the 1980s and 1990s, Jon Elster developed a new notion of the role of social mechanisms in sociology (Elster, 1986; 1989). Hedstrom and Swedberg write that "the advancement of social theory calls for an analytical approach that systematically seeks to explicate the social mechanisms that generate and explain observed associations between events" (Hedstrøm & Swedberg, 1998 : 1).

It is one thing to point out connections between phenomena. It is something quite different to point out satisfactory explanations for these relationships, which is what social mechanisms accomplish. A social mechanism tells us what will happen, how it will happen and why it will happen (Bunge, 1967). Social mechanisms are primarily analytical constructs which cannot necessarily be observed; in other words, they are epistemological, not ontological. However, social mechanisms are observable in their consequences. An intention can be a social mechanism of action. We cannot observe an intention, but we can interpret it in light of the consequences manifested through an action. Preferences can also function as a social mechanism for economic behaviour. We cannot observe a person's preferences, but we can interpret them in the light of the behavioural consequences that manifest themselves. Social mechanisms are, understood in this way, analytical constructs, indicating connections between events (Hernes, 1998).

Bunge says: "a social mechanism is a process in a concrete system, such that it is capable of being about or preventing some change in the system as a whole or in some of its subsystems" (Bunge, 1997: 414). By social mechanism here we mean those activities that promote/inhibit social processes in relation to a specific problem/phenomenon.

Material resources and technology are social mechanisms of the economic subsystem; power is a social mechanism of the political subsystem; fundamental norms and values are a social mechanism of the cultural subsystem; and human relationships are a social mechanism of the social subsystem. These system-specific social mechanisms interact with each other to achieve certain goals, to maintain these systems or to avoid certain undesirable conditions in the system or the outside world.

The difficulty of discovering social mechanisms and distinguishing them from processes may be partly explained by the fact that social mechanisms are also processes (Bunge, 1997: 414). For the application of social mechanisms, see the Boudon-Coleman diagram.

Social system

From a systemic perspective, social systems can be conceptual or concrete. Theories and analytical models are examples of conceptual systems. Further, social systems are *composed of people and their artifacts* (Bunge, 1996: 21). Social systems are held together (in systemic reasoning) by *dynamic social relations* (such as emotions, interpretations, norms, etc.) and *social actions* (such as cooperation, solidarity, conflict and communication, etc.). None of the social actions have precedence in the systemic interpretation of social systems, such as conflict in the case of Marx, and solidarity in the case of Durkheim.

Staccato-behaviour (erratic behaviour)

If organizations introduce too many change processes in succession too quickly, a phenomenon may occur called "staccato-behaviour".

If an organization does not deal with this appropriately, it seems reasonable to assume that workers will become tired, burnt-out and de-motivated. Perhaps most damaging to business, employees will lose focus on their primary task – what the business is designed to do. In addition, businesses will often experience that this leads to an increasing degree of opportunistic behaviour (Ulrich, 2013b: 260).

Strategic HR management

Strategic HR management is defined in this book as: *The choices an HR department makes with regard to human resources for the purposes of achieving the organization's goals.* This is analogous to the view of Storey et al. (2009: 3) and consistent with the definition we employ of HR management. This means that strategic HR management must be focused on the *micro, meso* and *macro-levels.*

There are many definitions of strategic HR management. For instance, use of human resources in order to achieve lasting competitive advantages for the business; management of the employees, expressed through management philosophy, policy and praxis; development of a consistent practices in order to support the strategic goals of the business; a complex system with the following characteristics: vertical integration, horizontal integration, efficiency, partnership.

Systemic thinking

Systemic thinking makes a distinction between the epistemological sphere (Bunge, 1985), the ontological sphere (Bunge, 1983a), the axiological sphere (Bunge, 1989, 1996) and the ethical sphere (Bunge, 1989). Systemic thinking makes a clear distinction between intention and behaviour. Intention is something that should be *understood*, while behaviour is something that should be *explained*. To understand an intention we must study the historical factors, situations and contexts, as well as the expectation mechanisms. Behaviour must be explained with respect to the context, relationships and situation it unfolds in. What implication does the distinction between intention and behaviour have for the study of social systems?

Interpretation of meaning is an important part of the *intention aspect* in the distinction. Explanation and prediction become an essential part of the *behavioural aspect* of the distinction.

In systemic thinking it is the link between the interpretation of meaning and explanation, and prediction, which provides historical and social sciences with practical strength. By making a distinction between intention and behaviour, the historical and the social sciences are interpretive, explanatory and predictive projects. According to systemic thinking, many of the contradictions in the historical and social sciences spring from the fact that a distinction is not made between intention and behaviour. The problem of the historical and social sciences is that the actors who are studied have both intentions and they also exercise types of behaviour; however, this isn't problematic as long as we make a distinction between intention and behaviour. By simultaneously introducing the distinction between intention and behaviour, systemic thinking has made it possible to identify, for instance, partial explanations from each of two main epistemological positions, namely, the naturalists and anti-naturalists (Johannessen & Olaisen, 2005; 2006), and synthesize these explanations into new knowledge.

Systemic thinking emphasizes circular causal processes, also called *interactive causal processes*, in addition to linear causal processes (Johannessen, 1996; 1997). Systemic thinking argues that to understand objective social facts, one must examine the subjective aspects of these. In systemic thinking, objective social facts exist, but they are often more difficult to grasp than facts in the natural world, because social facts are often influenced by expectations, emotions, prejudices, ideology and economic and social interests. *"Aspect-seeing"* is thus a way of approaching these social facts.

Emergents are central to systemic thinking. A pattern behind the problem or phenomenon is always sought in systemic investigations. Patterns may be revealed by studying the underlying processes that constitute a phenomenon or problem, *and the search for pattern is what scientific research is all about* (Bunge, 1996:42).

According to systemic thinking it is a misconception to say that the facts are social constructions. The misunderstanding involves confusing our *concepts* concerning facts and our *hypotheses* about the facts together with the facts. Our concepts and hypotheses are mental constructs. The facts, however, are not mental constructs. Social need, for instance, is not a social fact; it is a mental construct of, for instance, starvation. Starvation is a social fact. Social need is a mental or social construction. Not being able to read is a social fact. Illiteracy is, however, a social construction.

A *symbol* should symbolize something, just as a *concept* should delineate something. A *hypothesis* should explain something or express something about relationships. A conceptual *model* should say something about the relationships between concepts. A *theory* should say something about relationships between propositions. Physical or social facts are untouched by all these mental constructions. That one can through constructs change social facts, or that social facts are changed as a social consequence of using constructs, is neither original nor new.

The aim of theoretical research, according to the systemic position, is the construction of systems, i.e. theories (Bunge, 1974: v). The order in systemic research is thus: Theory–Analysis–Synthesis.

In the methodological sphere, the systemic position has its main focus on relationships, both in terms of concrete things, ideas and knowledge. Consequently, systemic thinking encourages interdisciplinary and multidisciplinary approaches to problems or phenomena.

The systemic position thus attempts to bridge the gap between methodological individualism and methodological collectivism, which is considered the classic controversy in historical and social sciences.

The perceptions that an observer has about social systems will influence his/her actions, regardless of whether the perceptions are true or fallacious. Systemic investigations start, therefore, writes Bunge *from individuals embedded in a society that preexists them and watch how their actions affect society and alter it* (Bunge, 1996: 241). The study of social systems from a systemic perspective for these reasons always includes the triad: actors–observers–social systems.

The observer tries to uncover a system's composition, environment and structure. Then the actors' subjective perception of composition, environment and structure are examined. In other words, both the subjective and objective aspects are studied. When we wish to study changes in social systems, from a systemic point of view, we have to examine the social mechanisms (drivers) that influence changes; both internal and external social mechanisms must be identified. This study takes place within the four subsystems: the economic, political, cultural and relational. According to systemic thinking, social changes occur along seven axes:

1   As an *expectation* of new relationships, values, power constellations, technologies and distribution of material resources.
2   As a result of our *beliefs* (mental models) about relationships, values, power constellations, technical and material resources.
3   As a result of *psychological elements*, such as: irritation, crisis, dis-comfort, unsatisfactory life, unworthy life, loss of well-being, etc.
4   As a result of *communication* in and between systems.
5   As a result of an *understanding of connections* (contextual understanding).
6   As a result of learning and new *self-knowledge.*
7   As a result of *new ideas* and ways of thinking.

Historiography, from a systemic perspective, has one clear goal: to investigate what happened, where it happened, when it happened, how it happened, why it happened, and with what results.

Systemic assumptions related to historiography and social sciences may be expressed in the following (Bunge 1998: 263):

a   The past has existed.
b   Parts of the past can be known.
c   Every uncovering of the past will be incomplete.
d   New data, techniques, and systemizations and structuring will reveal new aspects of the past.
e   Historical knowledge is developed through new data, discoveries, hypotheses and approaches.

In systemic thinking if changes are to take place, then the material will sometimes be given precedence; at other times, ideology, ideas and thinking are given precedence. In other contexts, there is a systemic link between the material and ideas that is needed to bring about changes. In such contexts, it is difficult and irrelevant to say what is the primary driver, i.e. the material or ideas; this would be on par with discussing what came first, the chicken or the egg.

The processes that drive social change, according to a systemic perspective, are the interaction between the economic, political, relational and cultural subsystems. In some situations, one of these four perspectives will prevail, whereas in others it will be one or more of the four subsystems that are the drivers of social change. In many cases, it is precisely the interaction between the four subsystems that leads to social changes.

In this context the systemic perspective may be described by saying that material conditions/energy, such as economic relationships, may provide the ground from which ideologies develop, but that these ideologies in return influence the development of the material. Whether material conditions/energy or ideology comes first is often determined by a historiographical punctuation process (Bateson, 1972: 163).

The systemic perspective balances historical materialism and historical idealism. It assumes that overall social changes are the result of economic, political, social and cultural factors, in addition to the interaction between material conditions/energy and ideas. Furthermore, a systemic perspective views any society as being interwoven into its surroundings (Bunge, 1998: 275). When a historian considers a historical situation – such as the massacre in Van in April 1915 – from this perspective then he is trying to throw light upon the internal working of a past culture and society (Stone, 1979: 19).

The systemic position attempts to view the relevant event in a larger context, in order to find the patterns which combine (Bateson, 1972: 273–274), because change depends upon feedback loop (Bateson, 1972: 274). Bunge says about this position: "By placing the particular in a sequence, adopting a broad perspective the systemist overcomes the idiographic/nomothetic duality ... as well as the concomitant narrative/structural opposition" (Bunge 1998: 275). This means, metaphorically, that the systemic researcher uses a microscope, telescope and a helicopter to investigate patterns over time.

Systemic research strategy is a zigzagging between the micro-meso and macro levels (Bunge, 1998: 277). Through a systemic research strategy the researcher has ample opportunities to use a Boudon-Coleman diagram.

Systemic thinking examines four types of changes:[6]

- Type I change concerns individuals who change history, such as Genghis Khan, Hitler, Stalin, Mao Zedong, etc.
- Type II change concerns groups of people acting together who change history. Examples of Type II change include the invasion of the Roman Empire by peoples from the north, and the Ottoman expansion into the Balkans between the late 1400s and when the Ottoman Empire was pushed back partly due to nationalist liberation movements in the early 1900s.
- Type III change include changes in history that are caused by natural disasters, such as the volcanic eruption that destroyed Pompeii. Climate change may also be said to an example of a type III change.
- Type IV change involves a total change in the way of thinking, such as the emergence of new religions, like Islam, or a new political ideology, such as Marxism.

The systemic researcher attempts to explore the relationship between the four types of changes. A single event is in itself not necessarily of special interest to the systemic researcher; rather, the focus is on the *system of events* of which the single event is a part.

All the social sciences are used in the systemic position to seek insight, understanding and to explain a phenomenon or problem.

Tacit knowledge

Knowledge that is difficult to communicate to others as information. It is also very difficult, if at all possible, to digitize.

The knowledge-based perspective

The knowledge-based perspective is defined here as creating, expanding and modifying internal and external competencies to promote what the organization is designed to do (Grant, 2003: 203).

The resource-based perspective

This perspective can be defined as the structuring and systematization of the organization's internal *resources* so it is difficult for competitors to copy them.

Theory

Here understood as a system of propositions (Bunge, 1974: v).

Notes

1 Asplund's motivation theory, a term we use here, is based on Asplund's research.
2 Asplund (1970: 55) refers to a similar phenomenon when he discusses Simmel. He points out that the norms that may have had a positive function during a historic phase become in a later phase dysfunctional.
3 Emergents appear if something new occurs on a level that did not previously exist on the level below. By emergent we mean: "Let S be a system with composition A, i.e. the various components in addition to the way they are composed. If P is a property of S, P is emergent with regard to A, if and only if no components in A possess P; otherwise P is to be regarded as a resulting property with regards to A" (Bunge, 1977: 97).
4 Emergents appear if something new occurs on a level that did not previously exist on the level below. By emergent we mean: "Let S be a system with composition A, i.e. the various components in addition to the way they are composed. If P is a property of S, P is emergent with regard to A, if and only if no components in A possess P; otherwise P is to be regarded as a resulting property with regards to A" (Bunge, 1977: 97).
5 North's action theory is a term we use here based on North's research.
6 The four types of changes are related to Bateson's (1972: 279–309) work on different types of learning, especially those discussed in his article *Logical types of learning and communication*.

References

Armstrong, M. (2014). *Armstrong's handbook of strategic human resource management*, Kogan Page, New York.

Asplund, J. (1970). *Om undran innfør samhället*, Argos, Stockholm.

Asplund, J. (2010). *Det sociala livets elementära former*, Korpen, Stockholm

Bateson, G. (1972). *Steps to an ecology of mind*, Intertext Books, London.

Bleuer, H. & Bouri, M. (2017). *New trends in medical and service robots: assistive, surgical and educational robotics*, Springer, London.

Bleuer, H., Bouri, M. & Mandada, F.C. (2017). *New trends in medical and service robots*, Springer, London.Boudon, R. (1981). *The logic of social action*, Routledge, London.

Boxall, P.F. & Purcell, J. (2003). *Strategy and human resource management*, Palgrave Macmillan, Basingstoke.

Boxall, P.F. & Purcell, J. (2010). An HRM perspective on employee participation, in Wilkinson, A., Golan, P.J., Marchington, M. & Lewins, D. (eds.), *The Oxford handbook of participation in organizations*, Oxford University Press, Oxford, pp. 129–151.

Brockbank, W. (2013). Overview and logic, in Ulrich, D., Brockbank, W., Younger, J. & Ulrich, M. (eds.), *Global HR competencies: mastering competitive value from the outside in*, McGraw Hill, New York. S. 3–27.

Bunge, M. (1967). *Scientific research, Vol. 3, in studies of the foundations methodology and philosophy of science*, Springer Verlag, Berlin.

Bunge, M. (1974). *Sense and Reference*, Reidel, Dordrecht.

Bunge, M. (1977). *Treatise on basic philosophy. Vol. 3. Ontology I: The furniture of the world*, D. Reidel, Dordrecht, Holland.

Bunge, M. (1983a). *Exploring the world: epistemology & methodology I*, Reidel, Dordrecht.

Bunge, M. (1983b). *Understanding the world: epistemology & methodology II*, Reidel, Dordrecht.

Bunge, M. (1985). *Philos sci and technology. Part I: epistemology & methodology III*, Reidel, Dordrecht.

Bunge, M. (1989). *Ethics: the good and the right*, Reidel, Dordrecht.

Bunge, M. (1996). *Finding philosophy in social science*. Yale University Press, New Haven.

Bunge, M. (1997). Mechanism and explanation, *Philosophy of the Social Sciences* 27: 410–465.Bunge, M. (1998). *Philosophy of science: from problem to theory*, Volume one, Transaction Publishers, New Jersey.

Coleman, J.S. (1990). *Foundations of social theory*, Harvard University Press, Belknap Press, Cambridge, MA.

Duncan, R. (1976). The ambidextrual organization: designing dual structures for innovation, in Kilman, R.H., Pondy, L.R. & Slevin, D. (eds.). *The management of organization*, North Holland, New York, pp. 167–188.

Elster, J. (1986). *Rational choice*, New York University Press, New York.

Elster, J. (1989). *Nuts and bolts for the social sciences*, Cambridge University Press, Cambridge.

Goleman, D. (1996). *Emotional intelligence*, Bloomsbury Publishing, New York.

Goleman, D. (2007). *Social intelligence*, Arrow Books, New York.

Grant, R.M. (2003). The knowledge-based view of the firm, in Faulkner, D. & Campell, A. (eds.). *The Oxford Handbook of Strategy*, Oxford University Press, Oxford, pp. 203–231.

Hamel, G. (2002). *Leading the revolution: how to thrive in turbulent times by making innovation a way of life*, Harvard Business School Press, Boston.

Hamel, G. (2012). *What matters now: how to win in a world of relentless change ferocious competition, and unstoppable innovation*, John Wiley & Sons, New York.

Hamel, G. & Prahalad, C.K. (1996). *Competing for the future*, Harvard Business School Press, Boston.

Hedstrøm, P & Swedberg, S.R. (1998). Social mechanisms: An introductory essay, in Hedstrøm, P & Swedberg, R. (eds). *Social mechanisms: an analytical approach to social theory*, Cambridge University Press, Cambridge.

Helfat, C. E., Finkelstein, S., Mitchell, W., Peteraf, M.A., Singh, H., Teece, D.J. & Winter, S.G. (2007). *Dynamic capabilities: understanding strategic change in organizations*, Blackwell, Oxford.

Hernes, G. (1998). Real virtuality, in Hedstrøm, P & Swedberg (eds), *Social mechanisms: an analytical approach to social theory*, Cambridge University Press, Cambridge, pp. 74–102.

Hewing, M. (2013). *Collaboration with potential users for discontinuous innovation*, Springer Gabler, Potsdam.

Johannessen, J-A. (1996). Systemics applied to the study of organizational fields: developing systemic research strategy for organizational fields, *Kybernetes*, 25, 1: 33–51.

Johannessen, J-A. (1997). Aspects of ethics in systemic thinking, *Kybernetes*, 26, 9: 983–1001.

Johannessen, J.-A. & J. Olaisen (2005). Systemic philosophy and the philosophy of social science. Part I: Transcedence of the naturalistic and the anti-naturalistic position in the philosophy of social science, *Kybernetes* 34, 7/8: 1261–1277.

Johannessen, J.-A. & J. Olaisen (2006). Systemic philosophy and the philosophy of social science – Part II: The systemic position, *Kybernetes* 34, 9/10: 1570–1586.

Kirzner, S. (1982). The theory of entrepreneurship in economic growth, in Kent, C.A., Sexton, D.L. & Vesper, K.H. (eds). *Encyclopedia of entrepreneurship*, Prentice Hall, Englewood Cliffs, NJ.

Merton, R.K. (1967). *Social theory and social structure*, Free Press, London.

Mosco, V. & McKercher, C. (2007). Introduction: theorizing knowledge labor and the information society, *Knowledge Workers in the Information Society*, Lexington Books, Lanham.

Miller, J.G. (1978). *Living systems*, McGraw-Hill, New York.

Nelson, R.R. & Winter, S.G. (1982). *An evolutionary theory of economic change*, Harvard University Press, Cambridge, MA.

North, D.C. (1990). *Institutions, institutional change and economic performance*, Cambridge University Press, Cambridge.

North, D. (1993). Nobel lecture, www.nobelprize.org/nobel_prizes/economics/laurea tes/1993/north-lecture.html#not2, (accessed 4.5.2012).

OECD (2000a). *A new economy? The changing role of innovation and information*, OECD Publishing, Paris.

OECD (2000b) *Economic outlook*, OECD Publishing, Paris.

OECD (2000c). *Education at a glance: OECD indicators*, CERI, Paris.

OECD (2000d). ICT skills and employment, working party on the information economy, Paris, 15 November, DSTI/ICCP/IE(2000)7.

OECD (2000e). *Knowledge management in the learning society*, CERI, Paris.

OECD (2001). *Innovative clusters: driving of national innovation-systems*, OECD Publishing, Paris.

O'Reilly, C.A. & Tushman, M.L. (2004). The ambidextrous organization, *Harvard Business Review*, 82, 4:74–81.

O'Reilly, C.A. & Tushman, M.L. (2007). *Ambidexterity as a dynamic capability: Resolving the innovators dilemma*, Harvard Business School Press, Boston.

O'Reilly, C.A. & Tushman, M.L. (2011). Organizational ambidexterity in action: how managers explore and exploit, *California Management Review*, 53, 4: 5–22.

Reinhardt, W., Smith, B., Sloep, P. & Drachler, H. (2011). Knowledge worker roles and actions – results of two empirical studies, *Knowledge and Process Management*, 18, 3: 150–174.

Roddick, D.A. (2003). The grassroots entrepreneur, in Elbæk, U. *Kaospilot A-Z*, Narayana Press, Gylling.

Stone, J. (1979). The revival of narrative: reflections on a new old history, *Past and Present*, 85: 3–24.

Storey, J., Ulrich, D. & Wright, P.M. (2009). Introduction, in Storey, J., Wright, P.M. & Ulrich, D. (eds). *The Routledge companion to strategic human resource management*, Routledge, London, pp. 3–15.

Teece, D.J. (2013). *Dynamic capabilities and strategic management: organizing for innovation*, OUP, Oxford.

Teece, D., Pisano, G. and Shuen, A. (1997). Dynamic capabilities and strategic management, *Strategic Management Journal*, 18, 7: 509–533.

Thota, H. & Munir, Z. (2011). *Key concepts in innovation*, Palgrave Macmillan, London.

Tushman, M.L. & O'Reilly, C.A. (1996). Ambidextrous Organization, California Management Review, 38, 4: 8-29

Ulrich, D. (2013a). Foreword, in Ulrich, D., Brockbank, W., Younger, J. & Ulrich, M. (eds.), *Global HR competencies: mastering competitive value from the outside in*, McGraw Hill, New York, pp. v–xxi.

Ulrich, D. (2013b). Future of global HR: what's next? , in Ulrich, D., Brockbank, W., Younger, J. & Ulrich, M. (eds.), *Global HR competencies: mastering competitive value from the outside in*, McGraw Hill, New York, pp. 255–268.

Ulrich, D. & Brockbank, W. (2005). *The HR value proposition*, Harvard Business School Press, Boston, MA.

Vadakkepat, P. & Goswami, P. (eds). (2018). *Humanoid robotics: a reference*, Springer, London.

Wang, Q-G., Lee, T.H. & Lin, C. (2003). *Relay feedback: analysis, identification and control*, Springer, London.

Wernerfelt, B. (1984). A resource-based view of the firm, *Strategic Management Journal*, 5, 2: 171–180.

White, J. & Younger, J. (2013). The global perspective, in Ulrich, D., Brockbank, W., Younger, J. & Ulrich, M. (eds), *Global HR competencies: mastering competitive value from the outside in*, McGraw Hill, New York, pp. 27–53.

Wilson, M. (2017). *Implementation of robot systems*, Butterworth-Heinemann, New York.

Winfield, A. (2012). *Robotics*, OUP, Oxford.

Wright, P.M., Boudreau, J.W., Pace, D.A., Libby Sartain, E.; McKinnon, P.; Antoine, R.L. (eds) (2011). *The chief HR officer: defining the new role of human resource leaders*, Jossey-Bass, London.

Winter, S.G. (2003). Understanding dynamic capabilities, *Strategic Management Journal*, 24: 991–995.

Zaltman, G., Duncan, R. & Holbeck, J. (1973). *Innovations and organizations*, Wiley, New York.

Index

Berlin Wall 5, 17, 34, 35

capitalism 1–28, 35–37, 60–62, 89
China 6, 12, 17–23, 27, 32, 34–35, 44
Cloud robotics 9
cognitive computers 46
collaboration 58, 70, 83, 97
collaborative system 59, 60, 69, 72
competition 5, 6, 11, 12, 20–21, 30, 31,
   35, 45, 49–50, 54, 59–63, 73, 80, 83, 97
complexity 28, 50, 69–71
context 13, 20, 27, 34–40, 44, 48, 54,
   64–68, 85–86, 91, 94
creative destruction 48, 49, 83
creative upswing 48
creativity 9, 42, 50–51, 73, 80, 84
cultural subsystem 57, 60, 66, 69, 72, 73, 90

destruction 8–9, 28, 48–49, 54, 60, 62, 83
Destructive wealth creation 40, 48–49
digitalization 13, 39, 64
disruption 15, 40–43, 55, 76

economic inequality ix, 23
economic subsystem ix, 20, 57–62, 72,
   73, 90
emergent 31–38, 58, 82–83, 95
entrepreneurs 8–12, 44–48, 76
European Central Bank 22, 27

fascist governments 21
feedback 1–2, 8, 46, 82, 94
Feed-forward 82
feudal capitalism 1–15, 60–62
financial capital ix, 5–6, 19–33, 58–62
flexibility 58, 68, 83, 88
flock 8, 24, 44
fourth industrial revolution, the ix, 1–18,
   32, 38–50, 53–54, 57–73

free trade 21–34
Front-line 41–43, 63–65, 73, 82
future workplace, the 2, 13

Global financial capital 25–27
global knowledge economy 27–28,
   63–64, 78, 83, 87
globalization 2–7, 11–32, 57–59, 64, 70,
   73–77, 88

ideology 10, 21, 23–27, 34, 72, 92–94
India 6, 12, 17–18, 23, 27, 34, 44
inequality 4, 15, 20, 23, 31, 36, 48, 75, 76
information 4, 9, 13–15, 25, 28–33, 39,
   41, 50–53, 71, 73, 74, 79, 81, 83–87, 95
informatization 1, 11, 13, 17, 18, 19, 22,
   23, 49, 50, 51, 52, 55, 57, 58, 74
informats 38–56, 73, 74, 85, 86
infostructure 28, 39–49, 83, 86
institutions 5, 10, 17, 18, 23–34, 53, 57,
   68, 71
invention 1, 14, 55
Iraq 19, 26, 64
Islamic State 19, 36

knowledge worker 2, 10, 11, 61, 87
Kodak 41, 49

leisure time 39–40

Mamounia 17–35
middle classes 4–6, 23–25, 47
migration 3, 6, 14–15, 18, 30

nation state 18, 58
neoliberalism 6, 26, 36
norms 28, 57, 67, 80, 84, 88, 90, 95

OECD 6, 11–12, 28, 44, 83, 87

policy 19, 49, 57–74
political subsystem ix, 20, 57–65, 72–73, 90
power system ix, 30–35
precariat 4, 10–16, 26, 31, 43–45, 48
productivity 4–13, 24, 35, 43–47, 67
protectionism 73, 74

Re-shoring 12–13
robot 1–10, 34, 38, 50, 52
robotization ix, 1–14, 35, 39–40, 47–48, 53–54, 64
Russia 19–22, 32

social crises 4, 14, 38–50
social storm 4
solidarity 64, 71, 80, 90

technology 1–9, 17, 23, 38–54, 64–70, 81
threshold value 1–2, 10, 46
time-lag 1–2, 7, 46, 48

unemployment 3–7, 12–15, 22, 46, 68
United States 6, 19, 22, 31, 38, 47

values 26, 28, 57, 68, 73, 84, 88, 90, 93

working poor, the 4, 13, 26, 31, 43, 45, 48
World Bank 22–25
World Trade Organisation 23